T0129529

REVIEWERS' COMMENTS

"Each man and wo/man must be true to the language of his or her own unique experience, but "what do we have here, Margo?" Can anything good come out of the mundane Indianapolis other than the poet S**IAM**? Jeffrey J. Phillips could be the Albert Einstein of Computer Science, the rebirth of another much needed interstellar **OM**niversal Carl Sagan, or the true **UN**veiling of the original Wizard of Oz who writes and reads like the prose of the late great Kurt Vonnegut. A cosmic poet who conveys his symbols and mystic heart through a technical vocabulary that he teaches you along the way, but whatever he's saying, praying, or conveying by way of his personal story, he's **DO**ing it in and through the power and wisdom of an ancient primordial Love that leaps out of this book to finger paint your innermost **BE**ing in kaleidoscopic colors only witnessed in a **SOUL**ular eclipse occurring once in a lifetime. More than a great computer scientist, Jeffrey J. Phillips, PMP and his new book, *Hi Gear, Lo Intensity*, is a must-read for anyone wanting to break free of this earth's gravitational force-field to experience the fourth dimension of this life and one's greater self."

S**IAM** [**S**haikh **I**brahim **A**l-Jahizz **M**'Backe]
Author of *Rain of Grace New & Selected Poems*

"Some men fight to be significant, Jeff simply is. Leading, giving, serving, celebrating his contributions, this compelling memoire shows integrity, humor and humility is alive and well in a man who really matters."

Rachel Bondi
CEO, Founder, Author, Speaker
MenMatter.com

Hi Gear,
Lo Intensity

Jeffrey J. Phillips

authorHOUSE®

AuthorHouse™
1663 Liberty Drive
Bloomington, IN 47403
www.authorhouse.com
Phone: 1 (800) 839-8640

Published by AuthorHouse May 30, 2020

ISBN: 978-1-7283-5818-5 (sc)
ISBN: 978-1-7283-5817-8 (hc)
ISBN: 978-1-7283-5816-1 (e)

Library of Congress Control Number: 2020906260

Print information available on the last page.

Brought to you by Adlayer Academy

Illustrator: *Mara Elizabeth Phillips*
Editor*: Dylan Stanley Phillips*
Marketing: *Diane Elizabeth Phillips*
Producer: *David Joseph Phillips*

This book is printed on acid-free paper.

Brought to you by Adlayer Academy

CONTENTS

SECTION ONE
HI GEAR

SECTION TWO
LO INTENSITY

DEDICATION

This book is dedicated to my loving wife of 30+ years, Mara Elizabeth Peláez Soto de Phillips. She is my muse, my best friend, and the single most important person in the world to me. Her strength and character are formidable, and her way of being never fails to delight, enthrall, and captivate me.

ACKNOWLEDGEMENTS

Many thanks to the myriad people who have provided suggestions, guidance, advice, friendship, and camaraderie along my journey. You are too numerous to mention, for I would be remiss to inadvertently leave someone out. I've appreciated all – you know who you are!

PROLOGUE AS AN EPILOGUE

His breathing was heavy and labored, the strength ebbing from his body with every passing moment. His mind darted furtively in and out of all the memories he'd stored over his long life, searching for something learned and lost long ago. He felt his wife and children nearby, but his eyesight was too far gone to see them. His twin sister was there, too, he could hear her voice barely audible above the receding din and cacophony that surrounded him.

"It's time," he heard a familiar voice say, one that he hadn't heard in many decades. "Come with me, you'll be fine." He felt the nearness of the voice, and then the memory of what he'd learned and lost long ago started coming back to him.

"I'm ready," he mumbled to no-one in particular but everyone in general, feeling even more lightheaded than earlier. "Let's do this thing."

And with that, he stepped off the ride, into the mystic, and the swirls of endless time enveloped him……

SECTION ONE

HI GEAR

The first section deals with workplace issues and experiences, based on empirical data - actual experiences through the eyes and ears of someone who was really there.

Best efforts were made to protect the identities of the actual persons. Some efforts are more successful than others……

CHAPTER 1

Bell Labs Blotto

The year was 1985. I had just earned my BSCS, graduating magna cum laude; I was feeling great, the future looked bright. I did a round of on-campus interviews with AT&T Bell Labs, and got hired into the Transmission Switching Systems division. My wife gave birth to our first child, a beautiful, bouncing baby girl. My new employer relocated me from the city to the suburbs, to be closer to the office, and I felt we were on our way to the good life. Life was so G-O-O-D!! Happiness abounded. There was no limit to the potential of possibilities to learn and grow, professionally and personally. My career in high-tech was just beginning......

My immediate supervision at the Labs was an Irish gentleman, keen of mind, slow of tongue, and absolutely glacial in decision making. I fast learned that corporations have a timeline to decision making that lies somewhere between watching an ant crawl from one end of the room to another, to sitting on the kitchen barstool waiting for the coffee pot to boil. My work at the Labs was very intriguing, I felt like a kid in a candy store, so many computers, so much software and hardware, so much to learn and experience and do. I worked in the computer center, with an Amdahl 5860 mainframe running UTS 370 Unix, several AT&T 3B20-S (simplex) minicomputers, an AT&T 3B20-D (duplex: wow, a dual-processor!) minicomputer, and a Digital Equipment VAXen farm as far as the eye could see: VAX

11/780, VAX 11/782, and VAX 11/785 minicomputers, the stalwart workhorses of the minicomputer era.

All the minicomputers were running on AT&T Bell Labs System V Unix. All the source code for the Unix operating system was readily and easily accessible. My officemate (a Chinese gentleman many years my senior) suggested that the best way to learn the inner workings of this famed operating system was by reading the file init.c line by line, painstakingly going over every function call and sub-routine, following all the links to system header files and other kernel and user mode modules, and reading that source code. Like I said, for a computer scientist this was like being a kid in a candy store. I sucked it all up, and read voraciously, and within months I actually thought I was getting pretty knowledgeable, and soon realized I was becoming a self-described Unix bigot......

One of the recruiting tools AT&T Bell Labs used on candidates was the OYOC benefit. For the uninitiated, OYOC was One Year On Campus, which meant that any eligible employee could apply for and receive one year's tuition in a computer science master's degree program at the University of your choosing. The best part was during this one year, you would still earn a percentage of your salary (I think it was like two-thirds, or something like that). What a deal! What a company! What a country! This was great. So after six months of working hard in the Transmission Switching Systems division at AT&T Bell Labs, I hit up my immediate supervision for the OYOC benefit. The conversation went something like this.

"I'd like to apply for OYOC." I queried plaintively during one of our weekly one-on-one meetings.

"Hmmm. I think it's only for eligible employees." was the response.

"Waddayamean? I'm an eligible employee aint I?" my naiveté must have been obvious.

"Well, I'm not sure, I'll have to check" my immediate supervision said, somewhat less than forcefully.

"Hey, sure, no problem, let me know." I replied eagerly.

A week later my immediate supervision informed me that I did not meet the definition of an eligible employee. I asked him why not. He looked me straight in the eyes, and very slowly and clearly enunciated that eligible employees were defined as women and minorities. Always quick on my feet, and thinking fast, I told him I was a Boston Jew married to an Hispanic Catholic, and the world didn't have too many of those, so wasn't I a minority, too? We both laughed half-heartedly, but the reality started sinking in.....

I wasn't eligible for this program, so I wouldn't be able to finish my master's degree as fast and with my employer's recruitment tool as I thought. What a disappointment! This certainly was a large contributing factor to my deciding to accept the position at this company. What a let-down to be told I wasn't an eligible employee. How could I possibly have foreseen that if I got hired I wouldn't be an eligible employee?

Lesson number one: note to self - always read the fine print. Bell Labs blotto. If they could dupe me with this, what else was I living under a misconception with at my employer? The honeymoon was definitely over now...... the kid gloves were off. Welcome to the workplace. Someone steeped in occidental philosophy would think "Don't get mad, get even". Someone exposed to oriental disciplines would accept the knowledge of the experience and learn from it. I chose the latter, and began contemplating next steps.

CHAPTER 2

PDU versus RFS

A decade before the browser wars of the 90s there was the internecine battle within Bell Labs about which technology to use for sharing network files in the subsequent release of UNIX - PDU (Portable Distributed Unix) or RFS (Remote File Sharing). System V Release 0, or simply System V, had been in use for quite some time. System V Release 2 was gaining new users every day, mostly people within the former Bell telephone companies, other telecommunications companies, and a smattering of university students, researchers, and some breakout companies trying to monetize the open software technology.

Of course, most bigheads weren't paying attention to what was going on with the System V side of the UNIX house, but rather were more interested in what was going on with the BSD (Berkeley Software Distribution) side of the UNIX house. The California regents had already decided their upcoming release, still under development, was going to use a brand-spanking new technology called NFS (Network File Sharing) if they could only iron out all the kinks. History proved that NFS had legs; it was good foundation to build from. But I don't think anyone ever talks about PDU or RFS anymore; at least I haven't seen any recent articles about it. Just another faded memory of a dust-up between warring factions in the scrap-heap of commercially unsuccessful software technology.....

I was still a young pup by Bell Labs standards, and it was my job to upgrade existing mini-computers with new hardware and corresponding new system software. Mind you, these were not the days of packaged software and automated installation scripts with visual aids. These were the days of make files and option switches and command line orientation. I had gotten used to sysgen'ing new kernels on VAXen and 3B20 mini-computers - maybe it was fun the first dozen or so times I did it, but it was getting kinda old by now. Learning how to tweak the tunable parameters to optimize the system performance was exciting, and creating new /dev entries was a tad tedious, but formatting and partitioning all those physically huge disk drives (the size of frigging washing machines!!) and migrating all those user data files really required attention to detail and fortitude. So opening up the six-foot tall, eight-foot wide, three-foot deep blue monster and installing an Interlan NI1010A ethernet network card into the VAX's central nervous system shouldn't have been a big deal. Popping the card into an available slot wasn't an issue - sysgen'ing a new UNIX kernel with the network interface software working properly proved to be more of a task than I had bargained for. Little did I know it would involve a couple of weeks of 18 hour days, more than a few all-nighters, and when all else failed, calling in one of the original coders of - you guessed it - a contender for one of the upcoming SVR3 (System V Release 3) networking technologies, THE developer of PDU.....

His name has long been relegated to those parts of my primary memory I can no longer access, but I remember he came from the development group in Denver. A ten-year Bell Labs veteran, he was very passionate about PDU, and was convinced this was the right network strategy to move System V into the future. During the days and nights we worked together, he told me about his ten years at the labs, all the interesting projects he had worked on, the brilliant people he had worked with. He explained that he was coming up on his ten year anniversary soon, within weeks in fact, and he was excited to see what would happen with his career. He said that at ten years, you either become a supervisory manager or a distinguished member of technical staff. If neither happened, then you knew you had no future at the labs and should either accept your fate as a solidly contributing MTS (Member of Technical Staff) with no possibility for promotion or else seek fame and fortune elsewhere, leaving gracefully. He was excited about his work with PDU, and saw it as his ticket to a cushy DMTS (Distinguished Member of Technical Staff) role with all the privileges and accouterments pertaining thereto. I was excited for him, and hopeful that he would achieve his dreams. I felt privileged to work beside this technical genius, learning so much about UNIX, network software, system software, and the AT&T Bell Labs corporate culture. Eventually we got everything up and running, our debugging and troubleshooting all those long days and late nights had paid off. Everything worked like a charm. The VAX 11/780 was now running a BETA version of SVR3 using PDU as its networking technology. We partied with the group, toasted our success, and this icon of a technocrat went back to his group in Denver. I wished him good luck, much success and prosperity in the future......

A couple of months went by, and we maintained email contact regarding the upgraded VAX 11/780, as well as new system software and other developments and timeframes for the SVR3 project. Since I worked in an applied research division (Transmission Switching Systems), not a basic research division like the UNIX development group, I used all my contacts to find out what was going on with SVR3, and my Denver friend had a lot of good inside information.

Eventually I finally got bold enough to ask him how his 10-year review went.....

I think we all know the end of this story. The PDU versus RFS wars raged on for months, and ultimately the RFS faction won out. My Denver friend and all his PDU efforts became a mere footnote in the annals of technology history. It was a huge disappointment for him, and was probably one of the causes for him to reach his 10 year career point without getting promoted to either a supervisory management role or the DMTS role he so coveted. Within six months he was sniffing around for other companies to work at, and within a year he was gone. I haven't heard from him since. He probably landed a good job at one of those networking companies that were starting to sprout up like weeds, Novell, Banyan, maybe something like that. I really never knew for sure. We lost touch. But I will always remember that time, when I worked at the feet of a genius, cutting my technical chops on networking systems software and hardware, on the big iron, before automated install scripts and visual aids and support hotlines, before the browser wars..... during the internecine battle within Bell Labs over PDU versus RFS.....

CHAPTER 3

Bourne Again

Matt Damon has done a few cool movies that I like a lot, action packed with twists and turns. Nice distraction from the daily grind, and good entertainment. My wife and I saw "The Bourne Identity" when it first came out, and even rented the DVD, so when "The Bourne Supremacy" came out, we headed to the theater and saw that one, too. I actually like this one even better than the first one, if that's possible. It gives new meaning to the saying "Revenge is a dish best served cold." Now there have been four Bourne movies, each better than the last.....

But when I hear the word "Bourne", I don't think of Matt Damon and movies. When I hear the word "Bourne", I think about a third generation programming language known by the cognoscenti as the Bourne shell. It's not a compiled language, it's interpreted, and so it's a lot quicker to prototype and debug your applications using Bourne shell. There were three flavors of shell in use in those days - Bourne shell, Korn shell, and cshell. The Bourne variant came standard with the distribution kit of the UNIX operating system from AT&T Bell Labs. Korn was an add-on you could easily obtain from other researchers and software developers within the former Bell companies, and cshell came standard with the distribution kit of the UNIX operating system from BSD (Berkeley Software Distribution).

While I started learning my way around the operating system with Bourne, I really got into the Korn shell in a big way. I started coding my prototypes and short projects using Korn shell. I even seriously considered naming our second child "Korny", but in retrospect I'm thankful my long-suffering wife talked some sense into me.

My professors in college used to say that we studied too many computer programming languages for the Computer Science degree. By the time I graduated, I had COBOL, Basic, RPG-II, Ada, Pascal, and C under my belt. I never used any of them in the real world except for C. But I guess all those languages helped me form an analytical approach to problem solving, heuristics, and algorithm development. By the time I learned C++ and more recently C#, fortunately or unfortunately I was no longer an individual contributor coding modules of a larger project, I led groups of project teams doing that. But I still remember developing this massive migration application for the computer center.....

I was into elegant simplicity at the time, and was starting to get bored, so I decided to code everything in Korn shell just to see if it could be done. We were running three different network topologies in the computer center - the superfast NSC hyperchannel, a reasonably fast AT&T version of ethernet called 3Bnet, and that good old standby serial interface, RS232. I wanted to make use of all available resources to migrate user data files between computer systems using any available media, either the three disparate networks or even the two different types of magnetic tape reels - 1600 or 6250 bpi (bytes per inch). My case and switch statements were tight, my error checking routines were flawless, and my conditionals never ended up getting linked to /dev/null. All using Korn shell syntax. After a couple of weeks of debugging and troubleshooting, I had taken a project that could have been done by a small team and easily dragged out to a few months and turned it into a one-man project completely prototyped soup-to-nuts, well-documented and defect-free. Korn shell ruled! How exhilarating. What fun. I accomplished what I set out to do. My immediate supervision was pleased. Some attaboys and pats on the back were received. To paraphrase a popular cartoon chihuahua from Ren & Stimpy, I felt like "We don't need no steeenkin' compilers!", even but for a brief moment. By using an interpreted language like Korn shell instead of a compiled language like C, I was able to prototype my project in record time with the desired results. It was a good feeling.....

So when I hear the word "Bourne", I don't immediately think of Matt Damon action-hero movies. I think of computer programming, and fondly remember the three different shells in use, and the time I used the Korn shell to prototype a massive migration application. But I bet there will be another sequel for Matt Damon. And it's sure to be a blockbuster like the first two, and Matt will surely look forward to being Bourne again.....

CHAPTER 4

Me 'n' the Missus

Me 'n' the Missus

I've mentioned her a few times previously, so I thought it might be a good idea to show her smiling face. After 30+ years of marriage, she still believes in me (silly girl!). What a saint - she's a real angel, my inspiration and my muse, and not least of all the mother of our three children. Bless her big ol' heart for putting up with a middle-aged, mid-career, cantankerous propeller-head like me.

CHAPTER 5

Nippon Electric Company

At the end of the nineteenth century, the Nippon Electric Company was founded in 1899 by Kunihiko Iwadare in cooperation with the Western Electric Company of the U.S. to become the first Japanese joint venture with foreign capital. Eventually Nippon Electric Company grew to become the manufacturing arm of Nippon Telephone and Telegraph, just as Western Electric Company grew to become the manufacturing arm of American Telephone and Telegraph. Telephones and switching systems were the bread and butter of these companies, and while NEC and Western Electric enjoyed boom times during the manufacturing age, NTT and AT&T similarly reaped a bountiful financial harvest from the cables carrying all these telephone calls......

After I resigned from AT&T Bell Labs, I worked at a telecommunications start-up focusing on voice-response systems for the financial and trucking industries. Going from the world's premier research and development organization to a struggling startup proved to be too much of a culture shock, and I soon found myself hired at NEC. When I first arrived, NEC had several U.S. divisions affectionately known as "the seven sisters" involved in different computer and communications and technology endeavors. I had the privilege of working in the computer division known as NEC Information Systems, Inc. where we developed big iron, minicomputers and PCs. A couple of years later, we merged with the home electronics division to form NEC Technologies, Inc. and focused only on PCs.....

The Astra XL product family ran on an NEC variant of System V Unix called Astrix, and used the Motorola 68020, 68030, and 68040 family of microprocessors as their central processing units (CPU). The BusinessMate product family had the capability of running DOS and Windows, but also ran SCO Xenix or SCO UNIX System V Release 2 and used the Intel 80386 and then the 80486 microprocessors as their CPUs. When I first arrived at NEC, my role was to teach NEC engineers and our customers' engineers everything I knew about NEC's flavor of UNIX - Astrix and our customized versions of SCO Xenix and SCO Unix. I developed a course curriculum that was useful on all the hardware platforms. It was fun flying all around the U.S., Canada, and Central America talking to engineers about what I was passionate about - Writing UNIX Device Drivers, Communications using UUCP, Bourne Shell Programming, and Unix System Installation, Operation, and Administration. I had a lot of fun experiences in faraway places trying to create a null-modem using pinouts 2, 3, and 20 (or sometimes even 7, 8 and 19) in an RS232C interface to illustrate running a *uucico* command from one BusinessMate or Astra XL to another.... factor in different revisions of firmware and peripheral devices, as well as interoperability issues between Motorola and Intel computers, and I was always kept on my toes......

I enjoyed teaching and traveling, but I yearned to be back in software development, so my immediate supervision let me code a bulletin board application system for the field engineers. I don't know if anyone actually used it or found it particularly useful when they could just call me up on the phone with questions, but I really enjoyed developing that system application..... before the days of automated bulletin boards (remember those BBS numbers?), before chat rooms and web hosting and instant messenger, I coded a complete system womb-to-tomb and learned a lot and had a great time doing it.

I sometimes wondered if a century earlier the founders of NEC could have foreseen that their groundbreaking work in telephony would spawn a worldwide computer and communications conglomerate that not only had the leading market share in Japan for personal computers but also sold over 15,000 products all over the world..... Or that their initial investment in technology would enable a computer scientist like me to play with so many different variants of my favorite operating system on so many different hardware platforms at the same time.....

CHAPTER 6

What the Hockey-Puck is a Keiretsu?

During my ten years working at NEC, I learned so many things about Japanese business practices, the culture, the approach to problem solving, and the philosophies. Although I never became conversant in the language, I was happy with the way I was treated and grateful for the time and attention I was given. I don't think I was alone in this feeling - I believe many other non-Japanese have experienced the same kind of respect and professionalism working in world-class multinational corporations originating in Japan like NEC. At the American companies I've worked at, I've always felt like a number (as that old Bob Seger song) goes, but at NEC I felt like a valued individual. I think a lot of this feeling had to do with the concept of the keiretsu (conglomerate), and the kanrishoku (management class).....

The Sumitomo keiretsu emerged from the Sumitomo zaibatsu (monopoly) - all zaibatsu were banned in post-war Japan. At the core of a keiretsu is a bank and a trading company, and in NEC's case these were Sumitomo Bank, and the Sumitomo Trading (or was it Holding?) Company. The keiretsu counted on the loyalty of its employees and the cooperation of all its disparate business entities. The way it was explained to me by my immediate supervision, at any given point in time some of the keiretsu's businesses were profitable and some were struggling, so in synchronistic harmony the profitable ones always helped the struggling ones. This maintained balance and assured the continuing existence of the keiretsu as a whole.

"Cool!", I thought, "Why didn't companies in the U.S. think that way?" I pondered rhetorically, "Why did U.S. companies always seem willing to eat their young in a short-sighted attempt to increase this quarter's numbers, instead of take a long-term, more collaborative viewpoint?".....

By now I was familiar with the different ranking systems and pecking orders in various and sundry American institutions. The military world had its various forms of ranks, whether it was the Army's private, corporal, sergeant, lieutenant, captain, major, colonel, general or the Navy's seaman, petty officer, chief petty officer, lieutenant, commander, captain, admiral and all the interspersed nuances of each level. The business world too had its various forms of rank, from assistant widgetmaker, associate widgetmaker, widgetmaker, senior widgetmaker, principal widgetmaker, staff widgetmaker, assistant manager, manager, director, VP, president and all the various layers within each management level. So I had a good frame of reference from which to learn the Japanese parlance, which I'd like to share with you. I hope you find it entertaining and interesting..... Below are the ascending order of the anglization of the Japanese words, and my understanding of their meanings. Any mistakes or misunderstandings are entirely my own fault - and any resemblance to reality is purely coincidental.

kan-di-shoku ---> management "class" (degreed professional)

ka-ka-richo ----> assistant manager (typically around 30 years old)

ka-cho ----> manager (typically 40 years old)

bu-cho ----> general manager (typically 45-55 years old, most employees don't attain it)

bu-mon-cho ----> senior general manager

tan-to-bu-cho ---> area vice president

fu-ku-sha-cho ---> VP, Senior VP, and Executive VP

sha-cho ---> President

so-dan-ya-ku ---> advisor, consultant (old, pre-retirement, but not a board member)

to-ri-shi-ma-ri-ya-ku ---> corporate board member, director

jo-mu-to-ri-shi-ma-ri-ya-ku ---> corporate board member, managing director

sen-mu-to-ri-shi-ma-ri-ya-ku ---> corporate board member, senior managing director

I suppose it's possible that understanding a little bit more about Japanese business practices and culture may help you someday when dealing with international customers. Or maybe the big take-away is to be sensitive to all the different business practices and cultures extant in the business world today. When you are on a business trip to a far-away place, take the opportunity to understand and genuinely appreciate the people and their ways, and don't always assume that what you think something means in your culture may necessarily mean the same thing in another culture...... When you started reading this you probably thought a keiretsu was some kind of sport, I hope you now understand a little more about the concept and all that stands behind it.....

CHAPTER 7

Device Drivers: Polling or Interrupt Driven?

After a couple of years I was given a team, and led a half-dozen software development engineers in the System Software department on new BusinessMate and PowerMate product development initiatives. One of these projects involved a just-released version of the Intel 80486 microprocessor and NEC's customized flavor of SCO Unix. I helped some of my staff on writing device drivers for an OEM'd video display tube to replace the standard CRT, which used the serial port as /dev/tty01 instead of the video console port. Others I helped in the intricacies of the network drivers for TCP/IP and NFS and making sure the networking subsystem worked well on the new hardware platform. And one poor soul on my staff got the dubious distinction of figuring out why the system always crashed if loaded with more than 16MB of RAM - something to do with the memory software subsystem and a particular semiconductor chip we were using.....

But alas and alack, there are never enough software developers to go around when you need them, so I took on one task myself which caused more than a few all-nighters and many late evenings of diet cola and munchies from the vending machine. On this hardware platform that was still under development, the super I/O chip was integrated on the motherboard with some other glue logic, and for some unfathomable reason the damn thing would just freeze up and die every time someone tried to send something out to the printer port. Normally in a PC the parallel port used for printing didn't cause much of a problem, but now it seemed on this particular puppy it was going to cause much wringing of hands and gnashing of teeth....

Slowly but surely, all the other product development issues were being finalized and achieving closure. The new OEM'd display, which the marketing folks called "The NEC Multiterm" (kinda catchy, eh? Not.) was ready for release, the BusinessMate 486/33E was ready to be launched, and one by one the technical software issues were being resolved. Except for the damn panic traps on the parallel port. I dived into the kernel to look for where the problems might lie. I checked the order in which all the system's different device drivers were booting up in the /etc/rc directory. I looked at the installation scripts for the some add-on desktop publishing packages. I tested the port using DOS and Windows commands, and I still couldn't find anything wrong. It was only under our flavor of SCO Unix that it didn't work.....

None of my debugging and troubleshooting techniques seemed to be yielding any positive results.

The symptom was simple enough, easy to see. If you tried to print something, the system just shit the bed (that's a technical term, of course). It didn't matter what kind of printer was attached to the parallel port, there was an error message that spewed to /dev/ console and the system froze up, accepting no further input, and had to be re-booted. So I started looking at the specific IRQ (I think it was number 9, but it's too long ago to be sure) and how it was handled by the operating system's interrupt handler routine. The device driver written for IRQ9 was interrupt driven, and I noticed the state machine was fine up until it actually started receiving data. So I thought to myself, what if I changed the paradigm, mixed it up a bit, and caused the device driver to be polling rather than interrupt driven. There were some command line over-ride switches that could be thrown in the printer's application layer that called the device driver that could force it into a polling mode, so that it was waiting and expecting to receive data rather than sitting there doing something and getting interrupted. If I could make sure this would happen every time someone tried to print something, then maybe I could get the system to stay up long enough to print a document.....

Sure enough, several code modifications and some brief validation cycles later, the problem was resolved. By changing the SCO Unix parallel port printer driver from interrupt driven mode to polling mode, the system no longer crashed when someone printed a document and all was right with the world..... Who knew? Who would have thought that it would make a difference? Polling or interrupt driven? But it did. Device drivers. So compact, yet so complex. Go figure....

CHAPTER 8

Multiprocessor Mumbo Jumbo

I was having a great time in the System Software department, developing new boxes and customizing SCO Unix for NEC BusinessMate and PowerMate product lines. But fortunately or unfortunately the world was ordering more of these with other 32-bit operating systems on them. The customer demand for these boxes preloaded with SCO Unix was far less than that for preloads with Novell, Banyan or Windows. I saw this as a good opportunity to get some experience and exposure on the business side of the house, and for the next five years I worked in the company's Product Planning and Management organization....

My first projects in PP&M involved all 32-bit operating systems, system setup utilities, and EISA configuration utilities. This was new and different for me, getting to negotiate contracts and licensing agreements with ISVs and OEMs. Next I worked on large tower Intel boxes with the latest and greatest CPUs, graphics, and hard disks. This was great, because it combined my budding business acumen with my existing technical background. It was about at this time that the multiprocessor project came up..... By keeping my ear to the ground, taking a lay of the land, and understanding the intricate nature of the relationship between our marketing team in the US and the marketing team back at the parent corporation in Japan, I did not feel it would be successful. The US marketing team were focusing on products with volume, trying to get revenues up and business thriving.

The Japanese marketing team was focused on building showcase products. In the Product Planning and Management team, we set the direction and tried to ameliorate any disagreements between our marketing colleagues on both sides of the pond. The multiprocessor project seemed doomed to failure because of a disconnect between these two entities, and therefore I didn't want any part of it..... I voiced my concerns to my immediate supervision, but we were under direction to complete the project from the technical perspective and let the marketing folks figure out the marketing plan.....

For the better part of nine months I watched this product get developed from the sidelines. A miserable, suffering colleague had the unfortunate displeasure of having to ride herd over its development and launch. Every time the Japanese planning team came over to discuss, the US marketing team did their best to ignore this project and focus on better revenue generators. When the time came where all software and hardware development was completed and the product was ready for launch into the market place, there was a big blowup and disagreement..... I don't know how many millions were spent on this, but I sure felt sorry for the guys on both sides of the pond who had their career aspirations dashed because of its failure. I don't think even 20 units got sold..... At the end of the day, NEC's Intel multiprocessor PC running on SCO Corollary MPX operating system may have been a good showcase product, but it did not fare well in the marketplace.....

After all that time under development, all that multiprocessor mumbo jumbo and hot technology, and no compelling business arguments. No salesmen or marketers could demonstrate to customers any software applications which took advantage of the multiprocessor capabilities..... oops. More than a few heads rolled at the next re-organization. I learned a big lesson then: better to work on products that actually get sold and generate revenue, than work on some cool new whiz bang product showcase with dubious prospects of making budget. Multiprocessor mumbo jumbo or not, at that time it was still the simplicity and elegance of uniprocessor personal computers networked in small workgroups that were being bought in large volumes, and that was, after all, what paid the bills.....

CHAPTER 9

Let the Good Times Roll

Working for five years in the Product Planning and Management organization of NEC's U.S. computer division was an awesome, exhilarating, and eye-opening experience. I learned so much about computer and networking technology, product planning, project management, and leadership. I had the most fun I'd ever had. The people I worked with were intelligent, collaborative, and really enjoyable to work with. Sure, there were exceptions to the rule, every so often a bad egg showed up, but they usually didn't last long and they were the exception rather than the rule..... I've lost track of how many generations of server, desktop, and consumer personal computers I developed during this time frame, but I sure enjoyed the work and the people. It was exciting and rewarding. The good times had arrived....

The side benefits were great, too - many business trips to visit strategic technology partners, prospective vendors, hardware suppliers, and independent software vendors in California, Washington, Texas, Florida and other places. These road trips usually involved travelling with other team members from marketing and purchasing groups, and everyone had such a great team spirit. We all worked well together. I remember this one trip during the late fall or early winter, we were trying to confirm our selection of some specific components and manufacturers on the next generation of consumer desktop personal computers. Everybody wanted to get in on the action, all the different department heads wanted to have representation, nobody wanted to feel left out. So there we were, at some swank dinner restaurant by the marina in some nondescript seaside town in Southern California - fourteen NEC engineers, product planners, project managers, marketers, and purchasers, and only two salesmen and a lone marketing guy from the vendor. We were enjoying the warm weather, taking it all in after a busy day of non-stop meetings and negotiations. A few appetizers and pre-meals drinks later, I leaned over to my immediate supervision and whispered "We're picking up the tab, right? You're not going to stick them with a large bill like this, are you?" to which he replied "No problem, I'm sure our budget will cover it." So I guess maybe one or two engineers went overboard with extra appetizers (or something!), because the bill came out much higher than expected...... But we still picked up the tab, because we were ethical and didn't want the vendor to get stuck with an unfairly large restaurant tab just because we brought along "a few" extra experts to help close the deal.....

Another time I was flying between Boston and Huntsville, Alabama more times than I could keep track of. I was spinning up a contract manufacturing plant that would produce a new generation of consumer PC. We were talking tens of thousands of units a month in volume, so it was important that everything was done in accordance with NEC's policies and procedures and all the technical specifications were met. I'd already had previous trips to Huntsville where there were no cars at the rental car lots, even though I had reservations. What good is a guaranteed reservation if it can't be fulfilled with a car? I even had one trip where I checked into a hotel late at night, was given my key, and as I opened to the door to what I thought was my hotel room I saw two baffled middle-aged women sitting in their pajamas watching television looking horrified at the stranger who just opened their door! I don't know who was scared worse, them or me. but nothing prepared me for the following exchange at hotel in Huntsville at about 11:00pm on a week night.

"I'd like to check in, please. Reservations for Phillips," I said matter-of-factly.

"Yes, one moment please..... Oh, I see it here. Here's your reservation. Sorry, we don't have any more rooms," the man behind the front desk said.

"But I have a guaranteed reservation," I said, "its guaranteed."

"Yes, well, I'm terribly sorry, but we don't have any more rooms," he replied.

"There must be some mistake, I have a guaranteed reservation that's guaranteed for late arrivals," I offered hopefully.

"I understand that, sir," the front desk clerk said, "but I'm afraid we can't honor it."

"Then what does having a guaranteed reservation mean around here?" now I was getting huffy.

"Well," he said, "it means you are guaranteed a reservation for a room, but I'm terribly sorry that we don't have a room to offer you, they are all taken."

"You have not a single room available in this whole wide big hotel?"

"No, sir."

"Not a single room? I find that hard to believe. What do you expect me to do? It's almost midnight, I just flew in after working all day, and I'd really like to get some sleep before my meetings in the morning," I suggested plaintively, figuring compassion was in order here.

"Well, actually, we have a conference room suite that has a sofa with a roll-away-bed. Would that work for you?" he offered.

"I'll take it." I replied, and I was off to a fitful night of uneasy sleep in a huge conference room on a small sofa bed. Lucky for me it had a bathroom complete with shower.....

So aside from a few bumps along the road, everything was rather pleasant. Cool products, cool work environment, cool colleagues. What's not to like? Let the good times roll...... I can honestly say those five years working in the Product Planning and Management organization of NEC's U.S. computer division were the happiest five years of my professional life so far. Thanks for the memories, everyone, you know who you are.....

CHAPTER 10

Westward Ho! A California Adventure

Nothing lasts forever, and all good things eventually come to an end. And so it was for my time and youthful exuberance in the Product Planning and Management organization of NEC's U.S. computer division. NEC had premium product lines, but coveted the larger market share of other U.S. PC vendors. In Japan NEC ruled the roost in market share for PCs, but in the U.S. that goal always seemed out of grasp. So ultimately, the unthinkable happened..... after years of rolling lay-offs to trim the fat and cut the deadwood, our division was now going to merge with - gasp! - the value leader in the PC food chain. Corporate chieftains back in Tokyo decided that combining Packard Bell's 37% market share with NEC's premium brand name and high quality products would result in larger market share and higher volume for all products. But no-one asked my opinion! No-one asked me what I thought of a merger between a value leader and a premium brand..... Of merging two corporate cultures so vastly different from each other any resemblance was pure coincidence.....

With the merger came redundancy in groups, and re-assignments to optimize human resources. In my case, over the years I had been promoted from product manager to senior product manager to product line manager heading up a staff of project managers and product planners for consumer PCs. The newly merged company didn't need two planning groups focused on consumer PCs, and since Packard Bell's strength was in consumer PCs, their group was chosen to stay in place. I was asked to go back to my roots in software engineering and lead a dozen engineers developing the software pre-loads for commercial and consumer desktop PCs. I accepted the new assignment, and went at it with gusto, refreshing my technical skills, leading my new team, and diving into Microsoft OEM Pre-Installation Kit (OPK) code with relish.....

This career move turned out to be quite fortuitous, because about a year later I received a call from a Sony recruiter, offering me the moon and stars to come to California and help them ramp up their new PC division. Discussions with my wife and kids ensued, I finalized negotiations with my new employer, and we were ready to embark on a new adventure. Westward ho! My ten year career at NEC had come to an end, but a whole new career awaited me at Sony..... And moving from Boston, my hometown and where we had lived for the past fourteen years, to the Silicon Valley in California, was an exciting adventure just waiting to happen. I, my wife and kids were all looking forward to having a California adventure..... little did we know all the peaks and valleys ahead of us.....

CHAPTER 11

Hey, Buddy; Can You
Spare Me a Dime?

When I arrived at Sony in 1997, I hit the deck with both feet running and was soon intimately integrated into the sprouting organization. Hiring was fast and furious as we went from a largely outsourced business model to bringing everything in house. It was a fun time to watch the organization grow. It was boom time in Silicon Valley, and everyone seemed to be enjoying their work, and their station in life......

I started out leading a small team of engineers from Japan who were on 2 year assignments in Silicon Valley. They were very dedicated and good software engineers. Within a short time I was managing a growing department with four sections, although my favorite section was software planning. In this role, I travelled to Japan frequently to dialogue with my counterparts in Tokyo. I usually brought one person with me, and usually this was an energetic and talented Ph.D. in computer science. We would hold detailed technical meetings with various groups in Sony's Shinagawa offices, and afterwards get on the subway system and go out to dinner. Note to self: things to do in Tokyo when you're not dead: see the sights and nightlife of Tokyo's various districts like Roppongi, Shinjuku, and Ginza; see the ancient temples at Asakusa; see the latest in gadgetry and technology at Akihabara.....

Sometimes it was formal business dinners, Japanese-style, and other times it was less formal and more casual. I remember this one time in the fall, when the Ph.D. and I arranged to take a bus tour of the city of Edo (Tokyo's ancient name) ending up with a dinner and watching a couple of hours of Kabuki theater. That was the best hundred bucks I ever spent (too bad I couldn't expense it!). I learned a lot about Tokyo and its different districts, its rich cultural history, and I got to see many parts of the city I hadn't yet ventured into. It was an awesome cultural learning experience.

Another time, I had sent several of my software engineers to Tokyo to work on a joint collaborative project with our colleagues from Sony Europe and Sony Japan. I had come over for a few days of high-level meetings about the project, and wanted to let my staff know they were appreciated and their extended stay away from their families in California did not go unnoticed. So I invited them to go to dinner in the Ginza district, to one of those famed steakhouses..... Well, we were walking around, taking in the sites, window-shopping, and trying to choose the best place to go to. It was getting late, and many of the places were already getting crowded. So we ended up at this smallish, hole-in-the-wall kind of place and feasted on Kobe beef steaks with all the trimmings.... Just a few sakes and Kirin beers were imbibed that night.....

A couple of hours later, when it was time to pay the bill, I confidently whipped out my corporate credit card to settle accounts. Imagine my horror when the waiter indicated the restaurant didn't accept credit cards. Huh? No credit cards? How can that be? This was the turn of the century in an advanced city in a technologically astute country, how could a restaurant possibly not accept credit cards? My mind racing, I tried to think of alternatives short of trying to communicate between my broken non-existent Japanese language skills and the waiter's less-than-perfect English language skills. And of course the sake and the Kirin beer weren't helping matters, either. Luckily, one of my engineers had gone to the currency exchange that day, and still had a lot of cash in yen to pay the bill......

Wow, close call. I honestly don't know what we would have done if he didn't have this cash hoard. What were we going to do, walk the streets of the prim-and-proper Ginza district panhandling like gangsta wannabe's? Can you imagine several foreigners there with their hands out, plaintively braying to passers-by "Hey, buddy, can ya spare me a dime?" I don't even know how to say that in Japanese.......

That night as I recounted the story to my long-suffering wife (see Me'n'the Missus in Chapter 4) on the phone back in California, she couldn't believe it happened. She couldn't believe I was stupid enough not to double-verify that the restaurant accepted credit cards beforehand, nor could she believe how we escaped a painful panhandling experience in a foreign land. But the stars were smiling on us that night, and all was well with the world....

CHAPTER 12

Seventh Generation Japanese

The Sony division I worked in was full of world-class engineers, marketers, and salesman. I felt honored to be a part of that team. Creativity was in high supply, and encouraged at all levels and in all disciplines. The procurement and operations folks were also highly talented and fun to work with. Imagine that, what a concept - purchasing staff with graceful social skills that weren't numbers-oriented and boring - how refreshing! It was truly a pleasure working with everyone on both sides of the pond......

In particular, I remember the VP of Sales at one year's annual sales summit. The meeting was held in the middle of the desert (gasp!) of the American southwest, at some nice resort teeming with golfers and tourists in addition to the large contingent of Sony sales and marketing staff. All the engineering department managers were invited, but not all of us could attend, so I was asked to represent one of my colleagues who would be receiving an award. Oh, man, I remember this incident as if it were yesterday......

I confirmed with my engineering director beforehand that the awards presenters knew that I would be accepting the award for my colleague who couldn't be there. He reminded me not to say a word to anyone about this, because no-one was supposed to know my colleague was going to win this award until it happened. So I kept it on the QT, even from my colleagues who were coming to the event with me. On the day before leaving for the event, I again confirmed, this time with my engineering vice-president, that the awards presenters would know that I was going to be accepting the award for my colleague who couldn't be there. The awards ceremony was on the second night, after the big dinner, so leading up to it I was confident that everything would go smoothly. I practiced my 3 lines that I was going to say over and over, to make sure I had it memorized and wouldn't look like a deer caught in the headlights. After all, there were a few hundred people in the audience that night, not only sales staff from all over the US but also executives from the home office in Japan.....

The lights began to dim. The awards ceremony had begun. The VP of Sales would call out the award, explain the great sacrifice and/ or accomplishment the awardee had done to earn it, and in the end call up the awardee to the stage. The protocol called for the awardee to say a brief thank you with a few words at the microphone, then shake the VP of Sales hand, then shake the President's hand, then get off the stage and return to their dinner table, glad-handing and receiving attaboys or attagirls all the way back to the table. I'm sure you've seen this scenario repeated at many such events.....

All of a sudden, I hear them call out my colleague's name. I bolt out of my chair with such suddenness that I appear to alarm my tablemates. I caught their perplexed looks in the corner of my eye as I strolled confidently toward the podium. Then I noticed the VP of Sales had this obviously perplexed look on his face as he saw me coming towards him, maybe he must have thought I was drunk or something, but I had a suspicion it was something far worse.....

You see, what I neglected to mention heretofore was that my colleague's name was a quite obviously Japanese-sounding name, and I was just as quite obviously not Japanese, having quite obviously non-Japanese facial features and physiology. As I approached the stage, the presenter made some wise-crack about me being a Seventh Generation Japanese in America, and everybody laughed at my expense. It was as this laughter was dying down that I reached the podium. Inside myself I was mortified, but I was determined to complete the task I had been directed no matter what the consequences. I got up on the stage, and took the trophy out of his hands as a stupefied HR director looked on dumbfounded. As I shook hands with the President, he smiled at me and said *en sotto voce* only he and I could hear "Jeff, what are you doing here?". It was one of those awkward prolonged moments in time, as I answered "Didn't they tell you? I'm supposed to accept this for him." The President smiled wisely and knowingly as we had one of those awkward longer-than-usual handshaking moments, as it was clear to me no-one had gotten the word to him. As I said my 3 sentences (which I had practiced over and over) at the microphone, the HR director and VP of Sales edged closer to me and whispered "That's enough, Jeff, now go sit down." Defiantly, I stayed at the microphone until I had squeezed out every last word I had so painstakingly practiced, then slowly turned around and gave them a dark, cold look that would stop a moose at mating time. I slowly sauntered off the stage and back to my table, vowing to have a little discussion with my engineering director and engineering vice-president about communications and follow-through.....

CHAPTER 13

Tiger Team

Working at Sony was a lot of fun, and there was remarkable synergy between divisions. Nowhere was this more evident than during the time Sony Pictures Entertainment (SPE) was getting ready to release the latest Godzilla blockbuster movie, and my division, Sony Information Technologies of America (ITA) was getting ready to release the first generation of the VAIO 505 laptop computer. Many newer Sony movies have exceeded Godzilla's popularity and box-office appeal, and many newer computers have exceeded the original VAIO 505's technical specifications, performance and sex-appeal, but back in the day, this was an exquisite opportunity for cross-marketing and leveraging Sony properties.

Minds much greater than mine came up with the idea that linking Godzilla (**BIG**!) and the VAIO 505 (**small**!) would allow both Sony divisions to leverage the marketing muscle of each other. My division formed a Tiger Team to bring all the different disciplines together to pull this off. I was selected as the engineering representative on the Tiger Team. At this point in my career, I was managing a team of over twenty software engineers as well as personally functioning as the program manager for the VAIO 505's software development and integration in the U.S. I was so busy I rarely had time to sit at my desk and answer emails! But I was having the time of my life.....

The Tiger Team was headed up by an advisor to the division's president. He was a personable chap from India with over twenty years' experience in the Silicon Valley at world-class technology companies in senior executive marketing roles. He and I hit it off very well, and during this project we became good friends. Other members of the Tiger Team included staff from product marketing, public relations, business development, sales, marketing communications, and operations. We met once a week for several months, and as we closed in on the launch date we started meeting more frequently......

As with most projects of this nature, where the pay-off is huge and the visibility is high, tempers would flare and disagreements would be hashed out, but it is a testament to the leader of this Tiger Team that everything was executed flawlessly. No scent-marking territoriality, ego-building pomposity, overwrought personality, overworked people, or just plain stress was going to get in the way of making this product launch the most successful in our division's short history. And so it was..... and so it came to be.....

On the engineering side my team executed flawlessly, and delivered a quality product on spec and on schedule. On the marketing side, they too executed flawlessly, and delivered one of the best marketing campaigns ever. All the other disciplines also came through with their deliverables - there were product placements, and advertisements, and commercials, cross-promotions with the movie, a favorable write-up in the Wall Street Journal by Walt Mossberg, and even a spot on some morning TV show in the gadget section. In fact, some of my favorite T-shirts still hanging in my closet are from this effort. On the front, the T-shirt has the big green Godzilla monster foot with the word "GODZILLA", and on the back the T-shirt has the diminutive VAIO 505 laptop with the words "SIZE DOES MATTER"......

But my favorite memorabilia from the Tiger Team remains something very special. The Tiger Team leader had it made as a token of his gratitude for all the members, for the time we spent together realizing the vision, making it happen. The plaque looks something like this:

Sony
Tiger Team
Special Recognition
Jeff Phillips

Your trailblazing creativity, dedication and spirit of teamwork paved the way for an innovative U.S. launch of the VAIO 505 SuperSlim Notebook.

With sincere gratitude and appreciation,
K.Ando
President
Sony Information Technology Company

SONY

Tiger Team
Special Recognition

VAIO

Jeff Phillips

Your trailblazing creativity, dedication and spirit of team-work paved the way for an innovative U.S. launch of the VAIO 505 SuperSlim Notebook.

With sincere gratitude and appreciation,

K. Ando
President
Sony Information Technology Company

Kunitake Ando became the President of Sony Corporation in Japan. I was invited to a dinner with him once, about a year later, and was happily surprised that he recognized and remembered my name. I felt honored yet humbled at the same time.....

I cherish these recollections, the T-shirts, the plaque..... they bring back fond memories of this time in my life, this project, the first generation of the VAIO 505 laptop computer, the Godzilla blockbuster movie, and the Tiger Team I served on..... I still keep the plaque on my desk, where I can be reminded of the experience every day and it will bring a sparkle to my eye. It sits right next to my Microsoft Ship-It Award, with a Bill Gates inscription - but that's a different project and yet another anecdote or two.....

CHAPTER 14

Interlude and Transition #1

After a few years at Sony, things were really heating up in the high-tech field in general and in the Silicon Valley in particular. It was a boom time for the economy, too. I now had 15 years of experience at 3 major league players in the high-tech field. So I decided to be adventuresome, step out of my comfort zone and be a risk taker. Opportunities abounded for me. In fairly quick succession, I became a director of software engineering at a multinational company (made my first business trip to Paris, way cool!), then VP of product development at an internet music appliance startup company (precursor of the iTunes business, we were a five years ahead of the market), and finally VP of engineering at a B2B ecommerce startup company. With dizzying speed I had accomplished my career objective, and was having so much fun and hard work developing software, hardware, and systems products with talented staff at a breakneck pace.

Looking back in 20/20 hindsight, I guess I knew in the back of my mind that it couldn't last forever. What goes up must come down as the Newtonian physicists always like to remind us. And so it was with the tech-fueled boom times at the turn of the last century. Everything seemed to fall like a house of cards - venture capital money dried up, the economy slowed into a recession, and hundreds of thousands of displaced engineers started showing up on the unemployment rolls.....

So what did I do? I did what any self-respecting, experienced, degreed computer scientist would do in troubled economic times - I went to work for Microsoft!

When I first arrived at Microsoft, it was an awesome place to work. Cool projects, cool people, and a cool work environment - life didn't get any better than this! I was on cloud nine, having the time of my life. For the first couple of years there, I kept wondering why I hadn't sought out Microsoft as an employer earlier in my career. Life was good....

CHAPTER 15

Release B

During the summer of 2000 in Microsoft's interactive television group, things were abuzz with anticipation. Our main customers were impatiently waiting for the production version of our software for high end set top boxes. Some months before I arrived, the head of the organization had promised everyone a trip to Hawaii if they released the product on time. They didn't, and now the engineers and business development people were anxious to put the finishing touches on the product and proudly roll it out the door. Release B was a step in the right direction.

At first I was aghast at all the different versioning schemes the group had invented as the delays rolled way past the customers' expectations. It seemed so patently transparent; who did they think they were fooling? They tried several flavors of Alpha and Beta to whet their customers' appetites, but none were really ready for prime time. Then they tried Beta 1, Beta 2, and Beta 3 to indicate they were getting very, very close to production-worthy code. When I arrived on the scene, they had just transitioned over to yet another new nomenclature - the alphabet - and had just released Release A and started working on Release B. I worked with the leadership to instill more engineering discipline into our processes, and create actual meaningful definitions for milestones. Up until now, there really wasn't great concurrence between the various technical disciplines (development, test, and program management) about crisp definitions on things like entrance requirements and exit criteria for milestones. The creative geniuses who held great sway over the organization felt that software code would just dribble out whenever it was ready to dribble out, and I felt that was a hell of a way to run a ship. So for Release B, I was determined to make milestones meaningful.

And so it was. Eventually, we were able to broker agreements between the disparate groups, and everyone worked long hours until finally, in November 2000, we happily signed off on Release B. We held release parties, and patted ourselves on the back- visible progress! We felt we finally were closing in on the last mile. We felt if we followed the same disciplined approach, the next release would be production-worthy. Finally, after so long, a product our customers could put into production use was just one more release away..... if only we could continue to agree with each other, stop internecine bickering, and all row the boat in the same direction...... we could see light at the end of the tunnel, and we hoped it wasn't an onrushing train.

CHAPTER 16

Ship-it Awards

When I was there, Microsoft had this really cool way of recognizing organizations that released **real** products to **real** customers. It was called a *Ship-it Award*. Maybe they still continue this practice, I don't know. But I hope so because it was a good one. Everyone who participated in the product development and market launch of a Microsoft product got one of these things. Mine has a nice grey marble base, with two black obelisks rising out from either side, with a glass etching in the center. The inscription on the glass reads like this:

> "Every time a product ships, it takes us one step closer to the vision: empower people through great software - any time, any place, and on any device. Thanks for the lasting contribution you have made to Microsoft history."

Bill Gates' signature is below the inscription, and a small bronze plate with the employee name is under that. On each of the black obelisks, the employee is encouraged to put the 25mm-by-40mm aluminum plaque containing the name of the product, the version number, and the release date. I'm sure the Ship-it Award's verbiage and appearance evolve over time, but it is still an inspirational tool for employees. In fact, when people interview, they are often asked how many Ship-it Awards they have, an indication of how many development cycles they have worked through. I still keep my Ship-it Award on my desk, right next to the Sony plaques I alluded to in a prior blog posting. My Ship-it Award reminds me of the four years I spent working at Microsoft......

After Release B, we were on a good roll. The technical teams started gelling very well together, and everyone knew we were on to something good. The program managers spec'd out all the features and APIs for the next release, getting buy-in from the software developers, test engineers, and marketing folks. The software developers coded the modules and subroutines necessary to support the marketing requirements. The test engineers performed quality assurance on the deliverables from the software developers, and when bugs were found everyone collaboratively resolved them one way or another. Some bugs need code modifications, others needed documentation changes, while still others were deemed not likely to occur in the real world, and yet others were left for future discussions.....

Finally, on June 1, 2001, we completed everything necessary and signed off on Version 1.0 of our product. True to form, just as we had hoped, the next release after Release B was production-worthy, so instead of calling it Release C we called it Version 1.0. We were so happy, ecstatic in fact! It had been a long haul - some of the engineers had been working on this product for a few years. It was very satisfying and gratifying for all of us in development. We only hoped our customers would be as ecstatic as we were. The customer landscape was changing, as the economy was diving deeper and deeper into recession, but we fervently hoped that our "showcase" customers would welcome our Version 1.0 product with open arms......

CHAPTER 17

Customer Landscape

Developing and releasing a Version 1.0 product at Microsoft is a near herculean task. Many great minds representing different disciplines with differing perspectives and agendas need to come together and agree that the software code is production-worthy. Comparatively speaking, subsequent versions are much easier to get out the door. After releasing Version 1.0 on June 1, 2001, we hoped our "showcase" customers would welcome the product with open arms......

Alas and alack; the downward spiral in the economy was taking its toll on our "showcase" customers. Slowly but surely, as the fiscal angel of death descended on their houses, one by one they started backing out of their commitments to us. We used this time of uncertainty to refine our product, even enhance it with some new features, and tweak it into the best possible state. We released Version 1.5 at the end of October 2001, thinking surely that would entice our customers to sign on the dotted line. We were all proud of the little plaque to attach to our Ship-it Awards, but the victory still seemed a tad hollow without real paying customers using our product. We continued to refine, enhance, and tweak, adding what we thought were surefire customer pleasers like PVR (personal video recorder, also referred to as DVR, or digital video recorder) features, and VOD (video on demand) features. We all worked smarter and harder and long into the night, hoping against hope that the business development and sales staff would garner design wins and customer satisfaction. Sadly, by the time we released Version 2.0 on April 19, 2002, the writing was on the wall. Not a single shipping, paying, customer had been won. The few customers remaining wanted yet more tweaks before they would consider the product ready, and frankly speaking we were all quite worn down.

To turn things around, a new executive was brought in to lead the future vision. We focused Version 2.0 on the last remaining hopeful customers in Europe and Latin America. We ramped up the staff for a new thin-client product for North America, and soon we were fastly and furiously specifying new features and roadmaps.

Finally, after much customization work, we signed paying customers in Europe for Version 2.0. Soon after that, after a complete overhaul and even more customized engineering development, we signed paying customers in Latin America. At long last, we felt good about what we had accomplished - a real product into paying customers hands. Life was good...... And still fresh development continued on, for the new thin-client product. We had high hopes that would really capture the hearts and minds of a much larger customer base. Customers are, after all, the main reason why products are developed, are they not? At least that's what I'd like to think.....

I learned many lessons during these years. As engineers we often overlook the changing customer landscape, but we do so at our own peril. A great product without a customer base cannot really be that great. Even if we create the most intricate, elegant, software solutions and provide compelling products and services, if we don't have the ability to market and sell them to real paying customers, our efforts are for naught. Ultimately, customer satisfaction is at the heart of a success - develop the right product for the right customer at the right cost and at the right time, and you'll have a winner, with many customers coming back for more. Develop a whiz bang technology just to show you can, and it may be a minor footnote in the dusty annals of some arcane museum somewhere. "Build it and they will come" only works in the movies. At least that's my story, and I'm sticking to it.....

CHAPTER 18

Interlude and Transition #2

After four years of working at Microsoft, the challenges were fewer and the excitement grew dim. I soon found myself yearning for new challenges and exciting new technologies. But where does one go after Microsoft? Is there life after Microsoft? After working for four years with some of the best minds in the software industry, what does one do for an encore?

As I engaged in this navel gazing exercise of introspection, I came to the realization that no existing technology company could meet my high standards of excellence, commitment, and perseverance. So I began to formulate an idea for starting my own company. On my own time, during weekends and evenings, I started a thought process that eventually led to the founding of my own company. I first talked it over with my wife of 22 years, and got her buy-in and support. Next I spoke with my 3 kids - two teenagers and a tweener. They encouraged me, gave me their blessings, and were just great about the whole thing. Then I started socializing my ideas for a new company with long-time friends who were uninvolved in my profession. Getting positive feedback, I wrestled with whether or not I should stay at Microsoft until my new company got off the ground, or else break off the ties that bind and start afresh. This was the most difficult decision-making process yet, because at its most elemental form, this decision involved the security and well-being of my family......

When I think of a safety net, I often conjure up images of trapeze artists in a three-ring circus, doing amazing feats of agility and gravity-defying stunts to thrill and amaze a captivated audience. Although most don't notice it, there is usually some webbing device, referred to as a safety net, underneath the area where the trapeze artists are working, so in case they fall they don't actually plummet to a horrifying death in front of unsuspecting little children munching on popcorn and candy cotton. If they fall, they are safely cocooned into the webbing device, and emerge unscathed, ready to get back up there and join their fellow trapeze artists. So the safety net serves the dual purpose of saving the trapeze artist from a gruesome mangled death, as well as not creating a traumatic event in the minds of the viewers. Very smart, that.

Not to mix my metaphors too much, but there is also this concept of free-falling when parachute jumping. In this context, free-falling refers to the brief moments in time between leaping from the aircraft and pulling the ripcord to release the parachute. It's an exhilarating sensation...... To keep your orientation, you must remember the colors blue, green, and brown. Blue for sky, green for ocean, and brown for land. By remembering these colors, even in a moment of distraction or panic, you can always orient yourself correctly to land upright on land. Which of course is much better than landing upside down in water...... Anyway, before you pull your ripcord to open the parachute, you are free-falling towards earth at an alarmingly fast speed, which causes the sensation of exhilaration. It's an exquisite feeling, a thrilling adrenaline rush of euphoria and pseudo-panic. Once you pull the ripcord and the parachute opens, you feel safer as you slowly float down to dry land. Your pulse returns to normal, you feel almost calm, compared to the previous sensation of free-falling......

As I mentioned before going off on a tangent about safety nets and free-falling, the most difficult decision-making process yet was whether or not to start my company before or after quitting Microsoft, because at its most elemental form, this decision involved the security and well-being of my family...... Do I free-fall without a safety net, or do I take the safe route and start my company in my spare time? What a fateful decision to grapple with! Greater minds than mine have struggled with this dilemma, no doubt, and I'm sure each person decides what's true for themselves in their own circumstances....

In my case, I decided I could not do anything half-baked. I could not start my company in my spare time. I had to work on it full-time. For I do things full-bore. When I decide to do something, I throw my passion, commitment, and energy into it completely. Was it risky? Sure! Was I apprehensive? You bet! Did my colleagues at Microsoft encourage me to stay? Of course! But in the final analysis, I listened to my deepest inner self. I went with my gut. I gave myself over to that indefinable construct of positive energy, threw caution to the winds, and just did it.....

I believed in myself. I thought to myself, "I can do this thing!" And so, I began free-falling without a safety net. I quit Microsoft, and founded TransformTec, a product development company and technology broker dedicated to converting intellectual property into cash. After 19 years of working at AT&T Bell Labs, NEC, Sony, Microsoft, and a couple of start-ups along the way, I took a leap of faith and jumped in feet first..... and became an entrepreneur - the founder, President, CEO, chief cook and bottle waster of TransformTec, Inc..

CHAPTER 19

Starting Out as an Entrepreneur in the Silicon Valley

If you've read previous postings in my Egalitarian Entrepreneur blog, then you know by now that I spent 19 years working for AT&T Bell Labs, NEC, Sony, and Microsoft, and a couple of startups, where I developed hardware platforms and software systems such as the NEC PowerMate personal computers, the Sony VAIO laptop and desktop computers, and Microsoft interactive television middleware. As a developer, I have a passion for engineering prototypes and developing systems. With this in mind, I founded TransformTec in the late spring of 2004. I saw an opportunity in my years at large corporations and small startups to capitalize on the fact that sometimes, really good ideas never make it to market. Some of these innovative ideas are emergent, while others are almost ready to launch. But in all cases, the idea generators cannot or will not bring these to market. I founded TransformTec to convert these intellectual property assets into cash. TransformTec is a product development company and a technology consultancy. We identified 41 acquiring companies in the telecommunications, multimedia, and consumer electronics space to which we wanted to market and sell. We analyzed these acquiring companies' strategic product roadmap needs, and fulfilled them with client's prototypes. In essence, TransformTec was all about converting intellectual property into cash.

That's the summary of why I decided to become an entrepreneur. But if you'll bear with me, I can tell you a little more below. Let me tell you 4 things about TransformTec. The leadership team we had in place, what TransformTec was, our paths to cash, and making money – what I like to refer to as "the TransformTec pipeline".

From the get-go, I knew I could do all the engineering tasks myself - like architecture, design, development, and program management, at least in the beginning. But for the nascent company to be successful, I also figured I needed a web presence, some marketing savvy, and some legal guidance. First I brought on board Dennis M., he and I go way back, he's been practicing law in the Bay Area for over 20 years. Then I brought on board Jim W., whose knowledge of crafting effective websites, and search engine secrets, has proven very helpful. Next I brought Chris S. onboard, who I've known for many years (including at NEC and Sony), and his marketing and sales skills are invaluable. I am confident being associated with these great talents as we bring TransformTec to the next level.

I can think of no better way to describe my company than by simplifying its fundamental premise: **Monetize intellectual property**. At TransformTec, this was done in two ways: (1) by working with idea generators to develop their idea into a prototype and then selling that IP asset to an acquiring company, or else (2) by brokering a fully cooked idea between an idea generator and an acquiring company. For my company, there were two paths to cash. But in both cases, we needed to understand the customers' needs - in this context that's the forty-one acquiring companies we were targeting. We needed to engage with them and figure out how to take some technology under development over here, to fill a niche in their strategic product roadmap over there. One path to cash is through developing products with idea generators, and the other is through brokering technology. Then it's simply a process of designing and developing a solution for the acquiring companies - preferably something that we've been working on with one of our idea generator clients! Regarding brokering technology, the path to cash there is through (1) cataloging intellectual property assets, (2) creating premium search services, and (3) offering topic sponsorships.

Finally, I'd like to explain the **cash cow** I built; my exit strategy was not to IPO or get merged or acquired. My exit strategy was to create a viable enterprise and lead that enterprise into the future, generating strong cash flow for stakeholders. I wanted to stuff the TransformTec pipeline with projects every year. Projects go in on one end, and revenue comes out of the other end. Sounds pretty easy, doesn't it? Well, it is simple, but let me tell you, it's definitely not easy! I intended to take on two projects the first year, with no sales activities or revenue generated. In the second year, my plan was to sell off the first two project's prototypes and intellectual property assets while simultaneously developing five more projects, and qualifying ten projects for year three. Ramping up staffing as needed and as appropriate is a skill refined from years of developing products. Conservatively guestimating each project to average $2.5m in revenues, by the time we would get to year five I was projecting $50m in annual revenues. I expected to sustain twenty projects a year, with $50m in annual revenues, into perpetuity. Hence, a **cash cow**.

Needless to say, things didn't work out quite like I had planned. But it was a great experience, and I learned a lot!

I'm very passionate about my work. In the first seven months of running TransformTec, Inc. I learned so many new things as an entrepreneur in the Silicon Valley, things I never could have learned before.

If any of this sounds interesting to you, I'd like to hear your comments. I would be interested in your feedback on my entrepreneurial ideas and my consulting company. I invite you to send us email at jeff@ adlayer.co. There are many issues facing entrepreneurs in the Silicon Valley today. I lived and breathed them in 2004 and 2005 when I ran my high-technology start-up company there..... and they are as true today as they were back then.

CHAPTER 20

Issues Facing Entrepreneurs in the Silicon Valley

There are many issues facing entrepreneurs in the Silicon Valley today. I lived and breathed these issues when I founded my company there in the late spring of 2004. To talk about all of them at once would be too lofty a goal, so in this chapter, I'm just going to focus on what I consider to be the top two issues based on my experiences. I'll ruminate on the rest of them in the next chapter. That's what's so great about writing your own book - I can write as little or as much as I want, whenever I want. The freedom to do so is liberating and quite energizing, I must say......

Sorry for going off-tangent, getting back to the issues facing entrepreneurs in the Silicon Valley today.....

I would have to say that money is hands-down the single most important issue. So **Issue # One is Money**, or really, the lack thereof. All the entrepreneurs I meet don't have enough of it, and all of them are trying to find creative ways to get more of it. I'm not talking about finding investment money, because each entrepreneur has their own "special" approach for getting funding, either from family & friends, angel investors, or from the last resort, vulture capitalists.... I mean venture capitalists. I'm referring to money from deal flow, money for work performed or expected to be performed.

I've talked to entrepreneurs at conferences and seminars, at networking events, at private lunches and dinners, at CEO forums, and in business meetings and phone calls, and the one thread that never fails to pop up in the same vein is the paucity, scarcity, and downright absence of money. I've had clients say to me "Zero budget, Jeff. Can we pay you after we've made our money?". This, after I'd worked on their account for six weeks. And I've heard clients offer "Money is tight. We'd like to pay you with a percentage stake in our company." That's great, but you can't put butter on it and stick it in a sandwich to feed your kids, can you?

One of the best ones I've heard is "We'll give you a success fee."

Okay, I'm game. From my Junior Birdman Decoder Ring that I pulled out of my kid's cereal box one day; I've learned that "success fee" is the 21st century way of saying "commission".

Isn't that what vacuum cleaner salesman and used car dealers work from, a commission? I never heard of engineering professionals working solely on commissions, have you? Commissions are great, when added on top of other compensation like salaries, bonuses, or consulting rates, but commissions-only compensation make monthly cash-flow difficult in my business niche environment, where sales lead times are often six-to-twelve months.

So money has got to be the number issue facing entrepreneurs in Silicon Valley today. Lack of it, and how to get more. **Lesson learned**? Always ask if there is a budget before spending any time with a prospective client! Don't invest too much of your valuable time with someone who has no intention of compensating you for it until too far out in the future.....

In my estimation, the second most important issue facing entrepreneurs in Silicon Valley today is gathering momentum for their start-up company. Going from a stand-still to 100mph in nothing flat is quite a feat, and you have to have the panache of a leader and the stomach for it. So **Issue Two is Gathering Momentum.**

One minute, your company doesn't exist, and the next minute, you breathe life into it, and you naturally need to spread the word about it.

First of all, how do you get people to take you and your business idea seriously? With hundreds of new companies coming on line, how do you make yours stand out above the crowd? How do you gather enough momentum to make your website attract eyeballs? With money in short supply, how can you get some visibility, ally yourself with strategic partners that won't ask for your first-born, and build deal flow to create a consistently recurring revenue stream?

All good questions, I would venture you'd agree with me here. So what are the answers? Well, in my experience, I've found that **gathering momentum is a function of the business relationships you build and the quality of the people you surround yourself with**.

As an entrepreneur and the CEO of my own company, I make the decisions about who I'd like to hire, about whether or not to join boards or associations, and even whether or not to go to certain conferences, seminars, or networking events. Early on, I found out about a business incubator and venture accelerator called TEN - The Enterprise Network of Silicon Valley. After meeting with their CEO, I was convinced he had the integrity and ethics for the kind of business relationships I find successful. I subsequently established business relationships with him and his staff, and even joined TEN.

This proved to be a good decision, resulting in solid business relationships with even more future potential. I also established business relationships with other CEOs and entrepreneurs in Silicon Valley that met my high standards of ethics, integrity, and relevance.

I don't suffer fools gladly, and I give short shrift to "flies" masquerading as entrepreneurs just waiting to take advantage of neophytes.

Then, too, instead of going out and incurring debt by hiring too many people and leasing plush office space before we had real revenue, I decided to bring on board a leadership team of three people to help me in their areas of expertise. Namely, product marketing & sales, business law, and web marketing technologies.

I had known these folks for many years, and I trusted them implicitly to do the right things for my company. So I surrounded myself with three people whose opinions I respected and who weren't afraid to give me bad news when necessary. **Lesson learned?** Creating a compelling website, talking about your company to everyone you see all the time, and proactively spending 125% of your time doggedly pursuing clients and customers - all these are extremely important and contribute to gathering momentum. And in my humble opinion, the business relationships you establish and the quality of the people you surround yourself with are the key for gathering momentum for your start-up company.

CHAPTER 21

Top Ten

Here are the Top Ten issues facing entrepreneurs in Silicon Valley:

1) Money, or the lack thereof!

2) Gathering momentum for your idea and/or company.

3) Staying power (or, how long is the "runway"?).

4) Influencing and motivating others to do as promised (or, responsibility without authority).

5) Separating the wheat from the chaff when taking on new clients and projects (who's hot and who's not).

6) Creating and maintaining deal flow (or, establishing your pipeline).

7) Turning prospective clients and customers into paying clients and customers (or, if they're not creating revenue today, are they really your clients and customers?).

8) Nothing attracts success like success (or, earning credibility one client at a time)

9) Repeat business (or, keep them coming back for more)

10) Financial and other metrics to determine your success, and learning to pass it on (or, it's never too early to share for other's benefit)

Surely these issues are applicable in other environs. But in Silicon Valley in 2004 and today - ten years after the dot.com bust - by paying attention to these issues and mastering them, the budding entrepreneur will have a higher probability for success......

CHAPTER 22

TechBA Inauguration

One day TechBA, the Mexico-Silicon Valley Technology Business Accelerator, held an opening ceremony for ribbon cutting in its new facility at The Enterprise Network's Sobrato Center for Innovation in San Jose. The distinguished sponsor was the government of Mexico's Secretary of the Economy, Fernando Canales. Other dignitaries at the VIP podium included:

- the Honorable Ron Gonzalez, Mayor of San Jose
- Bruno Figueroa, the government of Mexico's Consul General in San Jose
- Jaime Oaxaca, Chairman of FUMEC (Fundación México-Estados Unidos para la Ciencia, *translation*: Mexico – United Status Foundation for Science)
- Dr. William Musgrave, CEO of The Enterprise Network (TEN)
- Dr. Jorge Zavala, CEO of TechBA
- Alberto Herrera, CEO of Medida, a TechBA member company

The speakers gave impassioned speeches thanking the government of Mexico for its vision and support of TechBA. TechBA is a first-of-its-kind effort for Mexico in the Silicon Valley. Dr. William Musgrave gave the opening remarks, where he thanked the Sobrato family for their generous donation of The Enterprise Network (TEN) building, which houses TechBA and other TEN entrepreneurial companies. Dr. Musgrave also mentioned that TEN was asked to submit a US$2 million grant application with the U.S. federal government's small business administration office, and jokingly exhorted their representative in attendance to "please send us the check".

Jaime Oaxaca, FUMEC Chairman, gave an exceptionally compelling speech, saying how he had great credentials because he was born in Texas and knew every bar in Juarez, which got a round of applause and laughter from the guests. All kidding aside, said Mr. Oaxaca, he earned his engineering degree at University of Texas at El Paso and his business degree at Stanford University. Mr. Oaxaca acknowledged Mexico's Secretary of the Economy, the Honorable Fernando Canales, for his vision and proactive support of FUMEC and TechBA.

The Honorable Ron Gonzalez thanked the Mexican government's selection committee - which included FUMEC, Dr. Jorge Zavala, and several universities - for choosing San Jose and The Enterprise Network. Mayor Gonzalez mentioned it took less than six months from the time the decision was made until the time of TechBA's inauguration. He further mentioned that when he was first elected mayor of San Jose in 1998, he was the first Mexican-American to hold this office in San Jose. Since that took 150 years, he said, TechBA is setting a new high bar for the success of Mexican – United States business relations and ventures.

Secretary Fernando Canales inspired guests with his speech about technology commercialization on both sides of the border. Secretary Canales cited the reasons why the government of Mexico put so much faith and confidence in TechBA's mission, and set high expectations for the successes TechBA's member companies will accomplish in Silicon Valley and the United States.

Following the ribbon cutting ceremony, guests enjoyed a technical exposition of TechBA's member companies, and a buffet lunch. During the exposition, we had the opportunity to speak briefly with representatives of four TechBA companies. These were:

- Marcus Dantus, CEO of Simitel, which develops and markets IP based software for call centers
- Andreina Siller, CEO of Practum, which develops, trains, and sells project management software for small and large scale enterprises
- Guadalupe Sanchez, CEO of BrainUp Systems, which provides software development and application support services
- Abel Salazar of PESS, which provides power engineering services and solutions

About TechBA: TechBA is the first high-technology business accelerator started by the government of Mexico's Secretary of the Economy and administered by FUMEC, Fundación México-Estados Unidos para la Ciencia (translation: Mexico-United States Foundation for Science) in collaboration with The Enterprise Network (TEN), and assisted by several institutions of higher learning in Mexico such as: Instituto Tecnológico y de Estudios Superiores de Monterrey (ITESM), Universidad Panamericana (UP) and Instituto Politécnico Nacional (IPN). TechBA member companies are among the best and the brightest of Mexico's technologists and entrepreneurs.

As mentioned previously, TransformTec, Inc. was a California-based corporation that converted intellectual property into cash by focusing its efforts on developing software, hardware, and systems for the consumer, multimedia, and telecommunications sectors. The company turned ideas into reality by transforming technology concepts into products. Through a visionary business platform incorporating technology auctions and unique product development processes, TransformTec, Inc. redefined how new product markets were created and entered.

CHAPTER 23

Interlude and Transition #3

It had been a good ride, and I learned so many things in the year I ran <u>TransformTec, Inc.</u> But I eventually decided I couldn't continue to self-fund my company and I needed to "get a real job".....

So I set my resume up on the internet job boards, explored interesting opportunities hither and thither, and decided to accept a position in product planning and management with a UK-headquartered company focused on digital television technology.

I went to work in the Americas division, based in Boca Raton, Florida......

Perhaps the biggest single thing I learned during my time as an entrepreneur was about customers - without customers, a company cannot survive. My first major professional transition was from Boston to Silicon Valley. My second major professional transition was from the corporate world to the entrepreneurial world. This third major professional transition was from the entrepreneurial world back into the corporate world - a little older, a little grayer, a little balder, a little humbler, a little more forgiving of others, and yes, maybe a little wiser. In the past year I had learned about founding a company, accounting and financing for small businesses, motivating colleagues on a shoe-string budget, business development, marketing, public relations, and last but certainly not least, the importance of customer acquisition and deal-making. I combined those newly acquired skills and experiences with my existing technical skills and experiences, and forged ahead. Moving from engineering into marketing..... moving from Silicon Valley to South Florida.

The California Adventure was coming to a close, and the Florida Adventure was about to begin..... and my wife, our three kids and I entered it with relish, with gusto, and with eyes wide open. Its great starting afresh, my new colleagues were bright and team players, the company had lots of momentum back then, and I planned to be a major contributor to its continued success. Onward and upward, no looking back! The interlude was closing, the transition soon completed, as we slipstreamed into the next level in this game of life.....

CHAPTER 24

The Perfect Storm

Life in South Florida is never boring, that's for sure. In August 2005, I was kind of reminded of that old Humphrey Bogart movie about the people shut in a hotel during a nasty squall in Key West (does anyone remember the name of that movie?) Well, let me tell you that no sooner had I brought the wife and kids there and shipped my cars and household goods from the Bay Area, when all of a sudden - *HURRICANE KATRINA!!*

Literally two days after we moved into the Embassy Suites at Boca Raton, Hurricane Katrina came barreling towards Florida like the hot kiss at the end of a wet fist. My office closed early on Thursday, my younger son's middle school let out early on Thursday and was closed on Friday, and my older son's college shut down on Thursday and Friday. I was one of the last hold-outs at the office, and my young son kept calling me every 15 minutes asking me when I would get to the hotel because he was scared.

My wife and two older kids were holding down the fort, but my young son was frightened, I could hear it in his voice and pleadings for me to come home. I finally got to the hotel and we huddled around the TV for a while watching the storm news, then went into the atrium lobby and restaurant where we watched seas of people from farther south who had lost their electricity and/or their homes start checking into the hotel. Everyone was glued to their TV sets trying to get updates on the hurricane's ferocity and location. Thankfully, Boca Raton was spared any major damage, but just 30 minutes to the south in Fort Lauderdale was where Hurricane Katrina made landfall.

We drove through there a couple of days afterwards, and there were clean-up crews on the beach and in the streets taken care of downed power lines and felled trees. Sadly, 5 Floridians lost their lives. Worse, a few days later the storm headed up the Gulf Coast and nailed Louisiana, Mississippi, and Alabama before dissipating and heading up the continent. I've been watching the news about New Orleans in abject horror. My heart goes out to the unfortunate masses that are in such dire straits - the looting, the armed robberies, the depravity, the lawlessness. Literally speaking, this is a disaster of biblical proportions!! I saw an interview of a middle-aged man talking through tears as he explained he had to let go of this wife's hand as the flood waters tore him away from their house, and he hasn't been able to find her since.

Tragic, horrific, terrible, simply overwhelming.

Watching the news looked like a re-run of some B-movie zombie flick, it looked that hopeless and bad. I hoped and prayed that the government, charitable groups and civic organizations would mercifully help all these people get their lives back together. Indeed, many kind-hearted souls searched their hearts and sent their donations through their favorite charities.......

Meanwhile, as life slowly settled back into what passed for normalcy around South Florida, we adapted to our environs, and life went on. Work continued going well, my wife and kids made friends and learned their way around the neighborhood, and the Perfect Storm receded into the past......

CHAPTER 25

On Spamming

I had to turn off comments for some of my blog postings due to a spambot that found my site and inserted a bogus comment. If you're blogging and you haven't turned on the word verification feature or some other kind of monitoring feature, you should do that now.

Spammers suck, big time. Such a lazy way to get their messages out, with no cranial capacity at all. Morons....

If they only had a brain, they'd devise clever methodologies for reaching their target audiences instead of wasting people's time with unwanted invasive emails and pop-ups. I think they should all be rounded up and forced to watch George Orwell's 1949 movie "1984" and Fritz Lang's 1927 movie "Metropolis" until they refute technology entirely and go, Luddite-style, to live in a desolate deserted island somewhere where they can no longer inflict their double-digit-IQ spamming ways on decent hardworking folk..... but I ramble, so I'll stop here.

SECTION TWO

LO INTENSITY

This second section deals with personal observations, musings, anecdotes, and life lessons. All are based on the author's perspective.

Any basis in reality is purely coincidental.....

CHAPTER 26

The Last Time I Saw Elvis

You won't find any technical musings in this post, but I feel the urge to share it anyway...... It is said that a person's favorite music is typically what they listened to during their formative, adolescent years. I was 14 years old when I received a gift of the new album "Deja Vu" by Crosby, Stills, Nash, and Young from my widowed father's German girlfriend - she owned a pop-culture poster-and-music boutique near my high school, and was trying to win my favor by gifting me cool things. Her strategy didn't work (and neither, by the way, did their relationship) but the music remains and I have to acknowledge her role in bringing me to it...... And so it was that I listened to that album, and became hooked on their music. That's when this band became my favorite music to listen to. Over the years I've bought many albums by CSNY, but I've also bought albums by each individual in the band - David Crosby, Stephen Stills, Graham Nash, and Neil Young. Having a discerning taste for music, however, it was typically Neil Young's twangy falsetto, original harmonies, bluesy tunes, and compelling lyrics that brought me into the music store to make a purchase. Last month it was no different. Early in the month I heard an advertisement on the radio for Neil Young's latest album, "Prairie Wind", and literally within hours I was in Target paying for it at the cashier's. There are many great songs on it, sure to become classics, but unquestionably my favorite is "HE WAS THE KING - The Last Time I Saw Elvis". A tongue-in-cheek, finger-snapping, folksy, original composition about an everyman's last impressions of the great American music-legend-become-folk-hero, the song brings to mind a simpler time in our society when advertising wasn't so pernicious, our belief in society's idols was pure, and we could comprehend our idol's eccentricities without condemning them for their human frailties......

A couple of weeks after I bought the CD, I was going to meet up with some high school friends for a long three-day weekend. It's about 3 hours from our home in Boca Raton, Florida to Orlando, straight up the turnpike. I piled my wife and two sons into our white Surbuban (our daughter was visiting friends in California), made sure we had enough music, snacks and drinks for the ride, and we took off after work on Thursday night. Of course I brought my favorite seven CDs, but my family hadn't heard the Neil Young album yet (and I hadn't heard it enough), so naturally that's what I played the most on the slow, lazy, night time drive. We arrived at the hotel very late in the evening, so we hooked up with our friends on Friday morning and the fun began in earnest.

We met up with Steve and his wife Susie for breakfast. Since this was our first time to Orlando since the kids were infants, Steve gave us a tour of the city including some favorite shopping centers. Later on, Andy, Liz and Liz's daughter joined up with us back at the hotel. Soon, Rob and his wife Sarita checked into the hotel. Shortly thereafter, Diana arrived after an uneventful airplane ride from the DC area, and we all went to dinner at "Black Angus Steakhouse". Soon after that, Diana's daughter Risa drove up from West Palm Beach, and Liz's charming husband Mansour and their other daughter and her husband joined us. After dinner, we all went to Disney's Paradise Island, where lots of fun was had. We waited in line and got good seats at a 45-minute long comedy show (I don't think, though, that the Las Vegas reunions' "Second City Comedy Show" troupe has anything to worry about :-)), laughed at the comedians performing in "The Adventurer's Club", and danced our hearts out at "The Beach". Liz's daughter and son-in-law were pulled out of the crowd by the comics and entertainers on-stage, and everyone had a good laugh.

Saturday was time for more shopping at different shopping centers, hanging out at the hotel, schmoozing and getting to know each other better. Saturday night we went to dinner at "Fish and Bones" restaurant for a sumptuous meal while my two sons went to the Universal Studio's "Halloween Fright Night". After dinner we joined thousands of other merrymakers at Universal Studio's CityWalk. That was tons of fun!! We went in and out of several bars and dance clubs, grooving to the music, dancing, people-watching, drinking, and laughing the night away......

Late Sunday morning Eileen and her brother Dennis along with Dennis' son Aaron drove up from Tampa and we hung out at the hotel for a while getting caught up. Then Rob and his wife graciously hosted everyone at their beautiful home for lunch and an afternoon of fun and frivolity. Thanks to the hard work and superlative culinary techniques of Eileen, Liz, and of course Sarita, we feasted on chicken and pork adobe, lumpia, sticky rice, and all the trimmings - a veritable Pinoy Barrio Fiesta's potpourri of flavorful foodstuffs. Tasty taste bud ticklers, all of it! Since "the official oldest member" of our cadre, Steve, had just celebrated his birthday on Friday, a birthday cake was brought out. We sang a rousing round of Happy Birthday as Steve blew out the single solitary candle on the cake - perhaps a bit too much effort at his frail old age!! :-) Liz's husband Mansour even regaled us with a rendition of Happy Birthday in Persian, happily translating and explaining what the words meant. Good food, good company, lots of laughs, lots of reminiscing, catching up, and talking of the future. Someone remarked that only at a reunion of Manila alumni containing Christians, Jews, and Moslems can you serve pork without batting an eyelash, and everyone gets along famously. The camaraderie was palpable - you could feel the good vibes, fellowship, and caring that everyone shared......

As the afternoon turned towards dusk, one by one the cars were loaded up, tearful goodbyes were made, and people made their ways home. Back in the Suburban, driving down the Florida turnpike for the three hour trek from Orlando to Boca Raton, I turned my latest Neil Young CD back on the car stereo. In between refrains from "The Last Time I Saw Elvis," I could hear my two sons laughing uproariously and mimicking Steve's flawless fake Filipino accent "Galing! Galing!"...... until the next time I am fortunate enough to rejoin more of my old high school comrades for the next extended weekend of remembering what it was like being young and spry, growing up in that faraway place at that long-ago time......

CHAPTER 27

Lessons in Life – Never Give Up

It wasn't until I heard the song "<u>Basketball Jones</u>" by Cheech Marin and Thomas Chong on their first comedy album in 10th grade that I realized my sickness…..

Yes, I was hooked on basketball, and I had a basketball jones…… I started playing in the park in Urdaneta Village when I was eight, and carried on long after college and I was too portly and out of shape to do anything but set shots from the free-throw line and play HORSE. Even as an elementary student, I would watch the varsity basketball games at the high school, and idolize those big guys and their basketball prowess. "Height is might" versus "balya" shiftiness and caginess on the hardcourt, the games were always a lesson from which to learn. In my later years I went to see MBA (Manila Basketball Association) games at the Araneta Colliseum, studying first-hand the basketballer's craft. In my earlier years, after coming home from elementary school at 12:45pm to lunch, siesta, and homework, I would venture out into the blistering hot Manila sun, lovingly caressing my professional-size, rubber-composite (not leather, that was "maraming pera"!), orange basketball. I remember feeling the smooth dimples and sharp black lines as I would try to palm the basketball in my best Freddie Webb dribbling impersonation, quickly learning that the secret of palming the basketball for a pre-pubescent future basketball legend-in-my-own-mind lay in cupping the basketball closely between the wrist and the second joints of the fingers. It wasn't until high school I learned about that sticky-spray you could put on your hands that would allow you to easily palm the basketball with just your five fingers - rumored to be banned by our PSSAA (Philippine Secondary School Athletic Association) sports league. And it wasn't until senior year that I could actually palm the ball without any of the aforementioned subterfuge.

Many years of diligence and practice under the hot Manila sun, dribbling, passing, shooting, made me learn one thing - diligence and practice don't mean shit to a tree if you just ain't got it. Even if you have a basketball jones. I would practice almost every day, sometimes for just a half-hour if it was too hot, other times for a couple or three hours, when there were lots of people there and we had pickup games. By the time I was twelve I thought I was pretty damn good, so I tried out for the junior high school team, and didn't make it. Next year, I thought to myself, just keep on practicing, there's always next year. But I didn't make the junior high school team when I was thirteen either. With the tenacity of a bulldog, I just kept at it. More diligence, more practice, more hot Manila sun - you get the idea. So when I was fourteen I tried out for the high school basketball team, and came close to making it. I remember the coach calling me and this other kid, Chip Wesley, and telling us the final slot on the team was down to the two of us. I was 5'9", and Chip was 6'1", so I figured my odds were slim, but I gave it my all, I tried my best. It all came down to 10 shots from the free-throw line, the coach said whoever makes the most out of 10 shots gets placement on the team. I went first, and sank 7 of 10 shots, even though I was nervous as hell. Then Chip stepped up to the free-throw line; my heart was pounding, and I could hardly breathe as I was so excited my dream was about to come true. Seconds dragged by for an eternity..... then he started shooting. I couldn't believe my eyes, for in quick succession without so much as a by your leave, with steely nerves and brimming with confidence Chip sank one after another, hitting nothing but net, and commanded 9 out of 10 shots. I was a goner, a big lump in my throat, my eyes staring down at the cold, hard, wooden floor as I mumbled congratulations to Chip, thanked the coach for the opportunity to try out for the team, and shuffled off the court in shame. My dream was snatched from me again, as elusive as ever, yet I had gotten closer this time. Undaunted, with the perseverance only seen in dumb oxen and half-wits, I practiced and practiced, scrimmaging on intramural teams, playing for hours on the weekends, even watching NBA games on television, trying to learn the ball handing techniques and successful shooting strategies of Jerry West, Tom Bradley, John Havelchek, Mike Riordon, Earl "the Pearl" Monroe, Julius "Dr. J" Irving, Wilt "the Stilt" Chamberlain, Kareem-Abdul Jabbar, and all the rest of the basketball superstars of that long ago time and faraway place.

In ninth grade, I played left fullback on the varsity soccer team, and dreamed of making it "to the big time", and getting on the varsity basketball team. I had a great time with my soccer team mates, and since I had been playing soccer since second grade with most of them, it was something that I enjoyed and was half-decent at. I loved playing soccer, I enjoyed the game and hanging out with my soccer buddies, but I wanted more..... my basketball jones hit me hard, and I was a driven guy. Some days I would come home from varsity soccer practice, and - you guessed it - venture out into the blistering hot Manila sun at the Urdaneta Village park, still lovingly caressing my professional-size, rubber-composite (not leather, for it was still too "mahal"!!), orange basketball. Yep, I had a basketball jones, and I had it bad. By tenth grade I stood 5'9-1/2" (don't forget the 1/2!), 155 pounds, and I was ready for bear. I wanted to be on the basketball team so bad I could taste it. Alas and alack, my dream thwarted again, I had to content myself with being on the varsity soccer team - but this time, in tenth grade there was a consolation prize for me. I made the varsity volleyball team as well. Hey, I thought to myself, I'm one step closer to my goal. So when I wasn't playing volleyball or soccer, I was still playing basketball - more intramurals teams, pick-up games at the park, scrimmages at school in gym class, recess, or after school. I practiced and practiced and practiced, with a determination only certain people can relate to.

My high school junior year arrived, and my basketball jones was raging. I was glued to the TV whenever there was an NBA game, in or out of season (because of course back then there was no such thing as a "live" NBA game broadcasted from the states to Manila).

My skin was a leathery olive tone, from too many afternoons at the Urdaneta Village park practicing basketball under the hot Manila sun. There were some Saturday's when we would go to the school and play full-court basketball for four or six hours straight, using the school's official buzzer and scoreboard in the gym. That particular smell of the wooden floor after Mayo had polished and shined it brings back such fond memories, even now..... Pulling out the rafters so we'd have a place to hang our towels and street clothes, and to rest in between 12 minute quarters or breaks between games. Those were the days..... I had a basketball jones, and I had it bad. But like I said before, diligence and practice don't mean shit to a tree if you aint got it. So my junior year, I tried out and yet again failed to make the varsity basketball team. I was crushed, pretty much about dejected as a man can be without completely losing it. Again I had to content myself with being on the varsity soccer (I was now a starter at the center fullback or "sweeper" position) and varsity volleyball teams, my ever-elusive goal of playing on the varsity basketball team still escaping me. But with a glimmer of determination in my eye, and a gleam of hope in my heart, I forged on, practicing and practicing, never giving up. You see, I don't know if I mentioned this before, but I had a basketball jones.....

My senior high school year arrived, and I knew this was my last chance. Well, to make a long story even longer, I finally made it. My ten years of practice finally paid off.

At first I just rode the bench, but then Coach Phil Marocco started putting me in the game more and more. Finally I realized I achieved self-actualization on December 27th, 1973 when our varsity basketball team flew to play other Southeast Asian international schools in Hong Kong.

Our team wasn't doing too well in the tournament, we lost most of our games, but the coach put me in the final two minutes of the final game and I was as dumbfounded as the next guy when I hit a jump-shot from 25 feet out, achieving official status as "a veteran of international play" as Walter Euyang termed it.

We had some pick-up games with some of the local schools like La Salle and Ateneo, where I earned my chops and got street cred as a fledgling varsity basketball player, despite doing stupid things like once getting so confused in the heat of the game I grabbed a rebound and headed in the wrong direction - good thing I missed that undefended layup much to the crowd's howling delight and my teammate's disgust...... But I got better at playing in front of school crowds, saw more action in more games, and Coach Phil Marocco started counting on me more and more. I remember once at a PSSAA tournament at Clark Air Force base, we were getting our asses kicked, and the Wagner referees were favoring the home team, so Coach turned to me and Andy Mesmer and said "You guys are my 'hatchet squad'. Get in there, do the best you can, don't let them push you around - and if you have to rough 'em up on the backboards or on defense I won't hold it against you." That was fun. I almost fouled out, though.....

Then I remember the last varsity basketball game of the season. I remember it like it was yesterday, for, you see, I had a basketball jones. We were playing for third place in the tournament, we had been there all weekend, and we were pumped up. In the locker room before the game, as Coach named the starting line-up, I couldn't believe my ears as he decided to start me at right guard. I started in other games before, but none as important as this. This was the last varsity basketball game of my senior year in high school, this was a momentous occasion, and Coach was actually starting little ol' me! I had come a long way from that pudgy 8-year-old sweating under the hot Manila sun, shooting hoops at Urdaneta Village park, and I had achieved my ever-elusive, long-sought-after goal - not only had I made the varsity basketball team, but I got to start in some games and most importantly started in my last game. Nothing could be sweeter.....

The summer after I graduated high school, I spent two weeks at Purdue University at a basketball camp, courtesy of Mary and Tim Wallace, my father's long-time family friends. That was good, I learned a lot and saw the different styles from people all over the states. That fall and next spring at University of Denver I played intramural soccer and basketball, and clung to my memories of playing basketball in Manila.

In the decades since Manila and college, my basketball jones is largely in remission but every once in a while, it'll flare up. At my second house in Boston I put up a basketball hoop in the driveway, and in my second house in California I even had a 20'x20' concrete slab poured in my large backyard to play basketball with my sons. I sent one son to Golden State Warrior's basketball camp - not once, but twice! And I've been to my fair share of Boston Celtics and Golden State Warrior games, and I even took the boys to see a Miami Heat game with my good friend and former colleague Dudley Serravalle – hope to see more next year! Because I think it's possible that I still just might have a basketball jones......

CHAPTER 28

Faeries, Saints, and Sinners

Before I got married, I had a hobby which was a good creative outlet for me, and tons of fun. It all started when I was eight years old.....

Leona Lipton was casting a play about the valiant struggle of the Maccabees against their oppressors, and I was cast as Judah Maccabee (a.k.a., "Judah the Hammer", one of the greatest warriors in Jewish history). Now if you remember anything about Leona Lipton, at the time she was a very attractive young woman barely out of high school who could convince any guy to do just about anything. I was only 8, I'd never thought about being in a play before, but I was so awestruck at being asked and so willing to please this babe that I acquiesced. With wooden sword in hand, and with a costume made of plastic and rubber and old cloth, I spent my few minutes on-stage flailing away in mock battle with other 8 year olds and saying lines I could barely pronounce about topics I barely understood.....

In junior high school I did the lights and backstage work at the school's drama club. I remember Monty Swiryn directing me and Elliott Morabia, Richie Dayan, and Elico Musry in a 15-minute video segment called "The Man from T.E.M.P.L.E.", a parody on the television series "The Man from U.N.C.L.E.". That was too funny and very silly, but what do you expect from 12-year-olds with a 17-year-old director? I cringe when I think about the hammy acting, but still and all, I wish I had a copy of that 8MM film to show my kids how silly their dad could be..... In the drama club, I remember being up in the rafters operating the spot lights watching the older kids like Phil Pratico and Les Kayanan perform in "Damn Yankees", and "The Roar of the Greasepaint, The Smell of the Crowd". I remember being in the stage crew, and watching Sue Samara, Judy Chimento, Ann Mitchell and Marian Claassen practice for "Annie Get Your Gun". Then I played the never-seen, off-stage voice of Clifford Beers in the play "My Name is Legion", based on his ground-breaking mental health work "A Mind that Found Itself".

Soon after, I directed a one-act play for the drama club called "N for Nuisance" - I don't know if Hank Wasiniak will ever forgive me for that last performance, I hope he wasn't scarred for life.

And then there was "The Drunkard", or as it was formally known " The Drunkard or, The Fallen Saved, A Moral Domestic Drama in Five Acts". I played the leading man, the hapless Edward Middleton - an alcoholic who is egged on by the villainous Lawyer Cribbs and goes to the brink of losing family and fortune before being brought into the fold of sobriety by the virtuous Mr. Rencelaw.

Under the watchful eye of director Barbara Lawrence, my fellow castmates Erin Arp, Lee Cafege, Joe Dykes, Claire DeMyer, Debbie Hugel, Reg Maloney, Larry Jones, and all the rest of the cast and crew - we really had a memorable experience. From the barbershop quartet to the singing waiters, we really tore it up at the Army and Navy Club main theater pavilion. Some of my best high school memories are from those experiences with "The International Makati Players".....

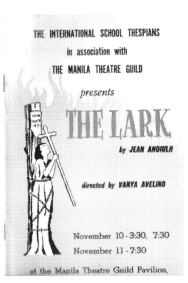

THE INTERNATIONAL SCHOOL THESPIANS

in association with

THE MANILA THEATRE GUILD

presents

THE LARK

by JEAN ANOIULH

directed by VANYA AVELINO

November 10 - 3:30, 7:30

November 11 - 7:30

at the Manila Theatre Guild Pavilion,

Later on we had a Russian drama teacher and director Vanya Avelino, who cast me as the Duke of Warwick in Jean Anoiulh's "The Lark", a modern version of the story of French heroine and later saint Joan of Arc. I fondly remember my castmates and crew - Debbie Guardian, Debbie Hugel, Kurt Baker, Freddie Gleeck, Maggie Wakeman, Kenny and Lori-Ellen Liss, Akbar Kazmi, Kenny Greenfield, and of course Lee Cafege and leading lady Erin Arp. I thought the material was kind of serious for a bunch of high-schoolers, but we went with it because that's how we rolled.....

Shakespeare's "A Midsummer's Night Dream" was next, where I can honestly say I had the weirdest role as "Flute the Bellows mender". What the hockey-puck is a bellows mender, anyway?!? Faery queen Sharon McClatchy was the hottest attraction of the show, although the other faeries, elves, and assorted mystical woodland creatures were just as interesting (if not quite as fetching).....

Playing the role of Nathan Detroit in the musical "Guys and Dolls" was a real challenge for me, because I couldn't sing or carry a tune to save my life, so director Ruth Butler asked fellow classmate, pianist and musical virtuosa Martha Shaffer to spend extra time with me learning my songs. I don't know if it helped or not, but I belted out "Sue Me" and "Luck Be a Lady Tonight" at the top of my lungs at the Philippine Cultural Center's main amphitheater in front of God and everybody and somehow managed to survive. Working on that play with Mary Jane Bruce, Tom Larson, Maggie Wakeman, Peggy Sullivan, Felino Menez, Barney Carville, Eric Moody, Phil French, Aldo Garollini and dozens of other castmates and crew was a tremendously fulfilling experience for a senior in high school that I still cherish today.....

THE COMMUNITY THEATER
PRESENTS

The Rainmaker

Directed by Frank Shepard

Starring: Jeff Phillips, Larry Salmon, David Thomas,
Jill Ahearn Sykes, Paul Baker, Dick Cañas and
David Thompson.

Friday 23rd, Saturday 24th, Friday 30th of April,
Saturday May 1st.
at the American Club, Vista Hermosa
Curtain Time 8:00 p.m. – Admission Q.3.

I did some dinner theater and community drama groups, acting in the Midwest and overseas, playing Tom Wingfield in Tennessee Williams' "The Glass Menagerie", Dr. Bradman in Noel Coward's "Blythe Spirit", several parts in Thornton Wilder's "Our Town", Tony in Tad Mosel's "Impromptu", Noah Curry in Richard Nash's "The Rainmaker", and even the sheriff in a low-budget b-movie called "The Kid".

CLUB AMERICANO
GUATEMALA, C. A.

3a. Calle 14-00, Zona 15
Colonia Tecún Umán

Tels: 691011 y 691758
Apartado Postal 414

Guatemala
November 6, 1981

DEAR VISITOR:

Wellcome to one of your COMMUNITY THEATER activities.

We hope you will enjoy with us and please let us
give you a list of our Cafeteria and Bar prices
(CASH ONLY)

HAMBURGUER with FRENCH FRIES	Q 1.00
HOT DOG	Q 0.50
PEPSI, COKE Etc.	Q 0.50
RON, VODKA, GIN	Q 1.50
WHISKY (Red Label) Cognac	Q 2.00
CIGARETTES	Q 1.00

THE MANAGEMENT

The Subject Was Roses

directed by Jeff Phillips

Phyllis Rantanan
as Nellie

Paul Baker
as John

Mike Evans as Timmy

Thursday March 3
Friday March 4
8:00 pm
The American Club
tickets Q2.00

Then I went ahead and got married. My future wife had watched me act in plays, even saw me direct one, and was always very encouraging. But after we got married she told me she preferred if I gave this hobby up, because she didn't want me hanging around with a lot of pretty women and (God forbid) kissing one on-stage. So after much wringing of hands and gnashing of teeth, I decided to respect her wishes and I haven't participated in drama activities since. I get my fill now by taking my wife and kids to the theater, and watch vicariously the actors and actresses exercise their craft.....

Drama for me was a hobby, never a serious professional pursuit, and it got my creative juices flowing. It was tons of fun, I met lots of interesting people, made many good friends, and I have many fond recollections to cherish. Those twenty years were great, from Leona Lipton and Judah Maccabee, to Noah Curry and The Rainmaker. Before I got married, I had a hobby which was a good creative outlet for me, and tons of fun. Although it all ended before I was twenty-eight years old, I have no regrets, just good memories and a loving wife and kids with whom to enjoy them.

CHAPTER 29

Requiem for a Teacher

It was one of those sweltering, hot Manila mornings, way back in nineteen-forgotten, on May 16th, 1974...... You know the ones I'm talking about, the unrelenting sun beating down on you with no shadow coverage in sight, with the sweat dripping down the small of your back and the tip of your nose, the acrid aroma of rotting fruit in the distance from some schoolgirl's thrown-away lunch from home, the pungent perfumed fragrance of balut wafting towards your nostrils like a bad memory of that Nasugbu beach trip with the SeaFront Teen Center - no breeze in the air, and you're trying not to look too uncomfortable as you sweat buckets like a stuck pig, trying to hide your glee that after twelve years of suffering through this tropical squalor you're almost finally free to return to the land of your birth......

She said "Russell wants to see you". She was a talking about Dr. Daryl Russell, high school principal. Since I was just daydreaming in the Senior Class lounge in between classes, pretending to be interested in the foosball game between Ahn Tuan Bui and Phil Adamson, I was a bit annoyed and felt put-upon by this interruption, but sauntered out the doorway anyway, down the hall and towards the admin offices.

"We'd like you to present the Outstanding Teacher's Award to Señora de Gaspar at the Honor and Awards Assembly", Russell said. "Walang problema, pare ko" I thought to myself, but somehow the words came out of my mouth as "Sure, Dr. Russell, no problem. What do I have to do?"

"When I give you the nod, walk discreetly up on stage and while I'm explaining the award to the crowd, I'll discreetly pass it to you. Just hold on to it, stand next to me, and after I finish talking, Señora de Gaspar will come on stage and you give her the award trophy and shake her hand." he explained.

Sra. Carman de Gaspar (left) accepts the Richard Spencer Award as outstanding teacher from Jeff Phillips at the Honor and Awards Assembly on May 16. The foreign language department chairman later thanked the student body for the award with tears of joy in her eyes. In response, the audience gave her a standing ovation as further evidence of the students' appreciation.

"When's this happening?" I queried. "In about an hour," he said. "Jeez, thanks for the heads-up, bonehead, 'tangina!" I thought to myself, but somehow the words came out of my mouth as "You can count on me, Dr. Russell." I beat it on out of his office, wondering how I was going to find time to sneak a cigarette outside the school gate near the old bookstore in time for my next class before the awards assembly.

As my body went through the motions of walking towards the gate and firing up a Kent, my mind started drifting to how I met Señora de Gaspar, how long I'd known her, my experiences in her class, and all she's taught me over the years.....

Like the many times we'd be watching old black-and-white movies of arcane, semi-pronounceable parts of Spain in the old A/V room before there was a Media Center, and Señora de Gaspar spoke in wonderment of how great Spain was and how we should all visit there one day.....

Or the times we'd be struggling through verb conjugation, vocabulary acquisition, and how stupid it felt to say "grathias" instead of "gracias", using the Castillian accent that Señora de Gaspar favored and tried to impose on us......

Or the time I just had just returned from summer vacation stateside, and was wearing a sleeveless, beige, ribbed, tank-top shirt favored by athletes of that era and she felt compelled to send me home to change my shirt because it was too "revealing" (bomba!!) and it would distract the girls in the class......

Or how I felt the difficulty of reading "Don Quijote de la Mancha" entirely in Spanish, and although I could read all the words and thought I understood the context, it wasn't until she explained the metaphor of chasing windmills that I felt my life on earth was somehow made more meaningful and my horizons were somehow broadened.....

She had a habit of doing that, Señora de Gaspar did, of broadening her students' horizons..... She wasn't just interested in teaching us new vocabulary, or correct pronunciation, or how to conjugate the most difficult "exception-to-the-rule" verbs and all those different verb tenses that were difficult to relate to in spoken English - plusquamperfecto, what the hell is that!?! (HINT: The Spanish "pretérito plusquamperfecto" verb tense is identical with the English "past perfect" verb tense.) You could really feel that Señora de Gaspar wanted you to experience life through the eyes of a fluent Castilian Spanish speaker, as if that would somehow transport you to a different world-view, a different perspective, a different way of living and experiencing life.....

You know, she was right. Spending four years in her Spanish classes in high school did broaden my horizons, taught me to be more appreciative of other cultures, and was really helpful later on in life especially when I went to live for a few years in Central America.

Her uncanny ability to reach out to each of her students individually, make each of us feel special in our own way, her genuine caring about our wants and needs and aspirations and likes and dislikes, her individual attention to every single student that came under her wing, whether for a short semester or for a few long years.....

I'll always hold a special place in my heart for Señora Carmen de Gaspar. I'll always remember her, and the impact she's had on my life. Vaya con Dios, Señora, vaya con Dios. Wherever you are and whatever you're doing, I know in my heart that you're teaching others, reaching out to others, making others feel good about themselves, and broadening their horizons. We'll all miss you, but the indelible imprint you've made on all our lives will ne'er be forgotten. Perhaps some time again we'll be sitting at your feet in that great classroom in the sky.....

Señora Carmen de Gaspar
Spanish Teacher
International School
Manila, Philippines

CHAPTER 30

Things My Father Taught Me

He was born on a sweltering hot summer day in the early 1920's, to an immigrant Englishman and a petite Bostonian. Growing up rough and ready in a working-class neighborhood, he learned many things from his father, a tobacconist with a shop in Chelsea, and other family and friends before graduating high school at the age of 15 and working for his brother-in-law at the tire store. Enlisting in the US Army Air Corps during World War II, he served as a master gunnery sergeant in the turret of a B25 before mustering out at the war's close and returning to Boston. Meeting and marrying the first love of his life in 1948, he soon moved overseas and became a very successful businessman and civic leader.

Tragedy struck when his wife of 10 years died, leaving him to raise 4 children on his own, and then again when his 12-year-old middle son David died of a congenital heart defect. After spending 16 lonely years as a widower raising his three remaining kids, he met and married the second love of his life with whom he fathered three beautiful and charming girls.

They lived an almost existentially happy existence in his adopted country, full of love and life and family. He shuffled off his mortal coils many years ago, and will always be remembered by his friends and family as a decent man, an honorable man, and someone who could be relied on in a pinch. Stanley D. Phillips was my father.

Dad was always busy with work or charitable civic events, so I relished any time I could spend with him. Saturday mornings were for religious services and Hebrew school, neither of which Dad attended, but he was adamant that we go and learn, for he felt we should be grounded in our heritage and learn from the community's leaders. Usually Saturday afternoons and Sundays were family time, going to restaurants and the movies. He didn't care what times the movies started, we'd usually enter the theater in the middle of a show and stay through the next showing until we got to the part we entered in. Funny quirk, that, but it did make me appreciate not to let the world's external time-table impose its regiment on me.

Dad would always light up a room when he arrived, he was an almost larger than life character, the life of the party, and everybody listened when he spoke.

And when it came to his kids, he would impart knowledge to us with terse yet pithy sayings that often left us puzzled with a quizzical furrow on our brow. Let's face it; he mostly talked in parables and metaphors that at the time would leave us scratching our heads, searching for meaning. As I age through my journey of life, I try to recall and fully grok their meaning so I, too, can learn to teach my children well.....

"You can lead a horse to water, but you can't make him drink." That was a favorite of Dad's, whenever he'd want us to do something that was important to him that we resisted. A signal of his frustration with our youthful recalcitrance, it usually meant the conversation was over with a shrug of his shoulders.

"You make your bed, and then you have to lie in it." This one was about responsibility, and taking accountability for our actions. Usually reserved for my older brother, who early on wasn't as responsible as Dad thought he could be.

"Never count your chickens before they hatch." This was especially apropos, as my middle brother David actually had an electric egg-hatching machine and our back-yard was full of little chickadees while David was alive. I'm not sure I've fully learned this one yet myself, as I'm usually overly optimistic about the future.

"You can't drink champagne on a beer budget." This was a good one that is intuitively obvious to the most casual observer, and is a word to the wise to not overspend above one's means.

"Never hit a woman." Period.

"Neither a lender nor borrower be." Obviously taken from Shakespeare's "Hamlet" written in 1603, this line spoken by Lord Polonius has an almost ominous portend of doom that far outweigh the six words within which it was given.

"Never judge a book by its cover." It took me many years to fully appreciate this one, but Dad laid it out for us in this simple way.

Dad always carried with him in his right trouser pocket a silver dollar minted in the year he was born. It was his lucky coin. A thing of beauty that was always kept in pristine condition, when questioned Dad would always joke that as long as he had it he would never be broke. I think behind the façade perhaps was a deeper meaning, a lesson to be learned, a connection perhaps, to his far-away homeland of Boston and the hot sweltering day he was born to an immigrant tobacconist Englishman and a petite Bostonian, growing up rough and ready in a working class neighborhood.....

AAP PRESIDENT'S WELCOME

STANLEY O. PHILLIPS

June 28, 1997
at "4th of July Hometown Picnic 1997"
SEAFRONT COMPOUND, ROXAS BOULEVARD
PASAY CITY, PHILIPPINES

100

AT&T

Global
Silverhawk

welcome you to the

4th of July

H o m e t o w n   P i c n i c   1 9 9 7

Saturday, June 28, 1997 • 2:30 to 7:30 p.m.
Seafront Compound, Roxas Boulevard, Pasay City

Presented by
American Association of the Philippines
American Women's Club of the Philippines
United States Embassy Club
United States Employees Association

STANLEY DAVID DOLPH PHILLIPS

Peacefully joined his Creator
on the 19th of July 1997

His bereaved wife, Aurora and **loving children,** Lee & Irene Phillips, Jeffrey & Betty Phillips, Joanne, Sharon, Stacey, and Stephanie; **grandchildren,** Jessica, Makaila, Sean, Diane, David, Dylan, Rosie and Maria request the pious readers to pray for the repose of his soul.

CHAPTER 31

Cousin's Daydreaming

It was a fun day in Sarasota on Sunday, 8th February 2009. A happy "**Cousins Day**". We drove from Boca Raton, Florida to Sarasota, Florida to hang out with my first cousins Alice Gochberg and Robert Paul, with their respective "better-halves" Harvey and Linda. Also joining us was their cousin from the other side of the family, Ruth Landsman and her mom Hannah Landsman. Betty and I brought Betty's mom Aurora and sister Candida.

We chatted and hung out at Alice and Harvey's house for a few hours, noshing on fruit, nuts, cookies and wine (Alice and Harvey are such gracious hosts!), talking about each others' families and getting caught up. Diverse discussions on world travels, far-flung relatives, and the family tree ensued, followed by the inevitable opinions on medical woes, a lively discussion on the economy, the global financial meltdown and of course esoteric, metaphysical, spiritual matters running the gamut from dream interpretation, numerology, astrology, kabbalah, and humanistic secularism. Good head-food, all!

Soon Ruth and Hannah arrived, and I bored the group with an encapsulated screening of a 1983 DVD of home-movies from Betty's and our first apartment as newlyweds including a birthday party Betty threw for my 27th birthday at Betty's mom's house.

No cousins gathering would be complete without a feast, and sure enough Alice and Harvey had made arrangements at the Palm Cafe and Grill. Such a wonderful meal and excellent service - Carolina and her husband really outdid themselves. Robert came up with a brilliant idea for all of us to "autograph" the menu, which we did - a copy of which I have regrettably failed to memorialize here.

The day ended as it began, with Betty, her mom and sister, and I driving back down from Sarasota to Boca Raton. It was a long day, but so memorable. Thank you all for a wonderful memory - let's do it again soon!

CHAPTER 32

Rabbis in the Workplace

Have you ever had a colleague at work in whom you confided that cheered you on during good times and offered solace and advice in bad times? I like to call this colleague "the rabbi in the workplace".

At the beginning of my career at AT&T Bell Labs, I was in a four-person office. One of the gentlemen with whom I shared this office was such a person. He was my first "rabbi in the workplace".

A Chinese electrical engineer seventeen years my senior, he always seemed to know the right thing to say, offering pearls of wisdom or epithets of consternation depending on any given situation. His family left mainland China during the Maoist revolution and settled in Hong Kong before immigrating to the United States. With a Baccalaureate in Mathematics and a Masters in Electrical Engineering, he held professorial appointments at a few universities before deciding UNIX system administration was his passion and ended up at Bell Labs. I still fondly recollect our many and varied conversations, and how instrumental he was in my professional growth.

At NEC my "rabbis in the workplace" were too numerous to mention here in this book, as I worked there for ten years and I don't want to offend by inadvertently omitting someone.

At Sony, a colleague with whom we shared a common boss was my "rabbi". A jovial and gregarious fellow, I still maintain tight communication with him to this day. He is a constant source of continuous support, enthusiasm, encouragement, and friendship. At Microsoft, a colleague who ended up being my boss for my last few months there, and another colleague with whom I shared a common manager for two years were my "rabbis". Good friends, we shared many personal and professional things in common not least of which were our spiritual, moral, and ethical value systems.

At Microsoft, a Brahman born in India was a close friend, and on many lunchtime walks we shared perspectives and traded philosophies.

At Pace, a colleague whose focus was on finance and operations was a frequent lunch and after-work drinks companion. Many a good conversation and pearls of wisdom did he share with me which I will always cherish.

At Technicolor, in and out of the office I met many sages from whom I learned much about Buddhism, Sufism, Kabbalah, Chabad, and several esoteric traditions. From a dearly departed high school friend in Miami who espoused the virtues of Buddhism, to a Kabbalah teacher in Los Angeles, to a Chabad Rabbi in Northern California, I am fortunate to have opportunities to learn and grow.

I feel blessed to cross paths with all these warm souls, and acknowledge their insightfulness and willingness to share with me. As my journey continues, I look back gratefully at my former "rabbis" and look forward to my future "rabbis", wherever & whenever you are.

And you? How many "rabbis in the workplace" have you encountered in your journey?

CHAPTER 33

The Land of Misfit Toys

The people I work with are important to me. Along with cool projects and a cool work environment, I think working with cool people is one of the most rewarding ways to spend your career.

But "cool" doesn't necessarily mean the best or the brightest. While many of the people I feel fortunate to have worked with were brilliant in their own way, a few were steady-Eddies - putting one foot in front of the other, steadily and diligently plodding ahead.

When the two types of people work together, shoulder to shoulder, achieving solid results, getting along well, then there can be a lasting impact which is just amazing to experience. I like to think of this concept as "The Land of Misfit Toys". Each type appreciates the other.

I think that comes from a movie I saw in childhood called "Babes in Toyland" starring Tony Curtis – some distant memory of laughing, colorful, magical toys. I don't really remember much about it, except some of the toys fit in and some didn't, but somehow and some way they all got along and were happy together.

Of course there is another much darker, more nefarious view about this concept. It is that all the toys that didn't fit quite right were sent away to a "special place", never to be heard from again. No-one ever really knew what happened to them, but the suspicion was they were destroyed or converted or otherwise met an unhappy and untimely demise.

You can choose to think of this concept of "The Land of Misfit Toys" in positive light - a bunch of misfit (and not-misfit) toys happily singing or working alongside each other, or you can choose to think of demise and destruction in a "special place". You choose.

As for me, whenever I think of those experiences, I get a twinkle in my eye and a bounce in my step.

Ever live or work in "The Land of Misfit Toys"?

EPILOGUE AS A PROLOGUE

Shari was breathing heavily, in the final throes of childbirth. Calm and demure, with a fire in her eyes that only a red-head can possibly know about, she and her husband had been preparing for this day for many months. Today was a sun-filled warm day on Cape Cod, and the pace at Barnstable County Hospital was starting to pick up as the dawn approached. Stan and Shari were tired yet excited about the birth of the twins, an excitement they shared with Shari's step-father Joe, after whom the twin babies were soon named.

"The first one's head is crowning," said the doctor excitedly, "one more push, you can do it!"

Stan whispered into his wife's ear "I love you, just relax."

Six minutes later it was all over. The boy was born first, the girl was born next - five minutes apart - just as light was dawning over Marblehead. The following decades of their existence would come to pass with wonder, enlightenment, joy, and sorrow, with a shared birth forging a bond holding the twins together sometimes better than others.......

ABOUT THE AUTHOR

Jeffrey J. Phillips, PMP® has worked at Fortune 50 and start-up companies for 30+ years. Starting his career in the early days of the UNIX™ operating system at AT&T Bell Labs, he then spent a decade developing innovative personal computers at NEC's PC division. Next he moved to Sony for a few years pioneering and developing their hard disk image process while bringing the first generation of Sony's VAIO 505 laptop to market. After working for four years at Microsoft's MSTV division, he spent the next two decades as a key leader on teams that collaborated on the planning, design, development, launch, manufacture, distribution and support of innovative set-top boxes and gateways while occasionally giving classroom instruction on Project Management as a discipline. Now, in between volunteer work at a non-profit organization and looking for his next full-time job in high tech, he enjoys creative writing, time with his wife and family, exploring spirituality, and living in northern California.

Printed in the United States
By Bookmasters